WITHDRAWN

THE TIME OF THE CUCKOO

THE TIME
OF THE
CUCKOO

A Comedy
by
ARTHUR LAURENTS

The cuckoo is a summer visitant to
the whole of Europe. It proclaims its
arrival by a cry heralding the season
of love... —*Encyclopædia Britannica*

RANDOM HOUSE · NEW YORK

Frontispiece photograph by Vandamm

MANUFACTURED IN THE UNITED STATES OF AMERICA

In Memoriam

LOOKOUT MOUNTAIN

The Time of the Cuckoo was first presented by Robert White-head and Walter Fried at the Empire Theatre, New York City, on Wednesday, October 15, 1952, with the following cast:

[In Order of Speaking]

SIGNORA FIORIA	*Lydia St. Clair*
EDDIE YAEGER	*Donald Murphy*
JUNE YAEGER	*Geraldine Brooks*
GIOVANNA	*Sylvia Gassel*
LEONA SAMISH	*Shirley Booth*
MRS. MC ILHENNY	*Jane Rose*
MR. MC ILHENNY	*Daniel Reed*
MAURO	*Jose Perez*
RENATO DI ROSSI	*Dino DiLuca*
VITO	*Ruggero Romor*

Directed by Harold Clurman

Setting and Lighting by Ben Edwards

Costumes by Helene Pons

SCENES

The play takes place in the garden of the Pensione Fioria,
Venice, in summertime. The action is divided into two acts,
with three scenes in each.

ACT ONE

ACT ONE

Scene I

The garden of the Pensione Fioria is a green oasis of quiet near the center of Venice, bordering on a small canal. A tree rises from the flagstoned floor; a dining section is under a vine-covered arbor; a high stone wall is also trellised with leaves. This wall borders a rio (a small Venetian canal) on one side, then angles to continue along the back of the garden. On the canal side the wall parts for a small door and three steps leading down to a gondola landing. Just above and beyond the right-angled corner is visible part of a small stone footbridge which crosses the canal.

Behind the back wall, there is an unseen, narrow calle (street) and the back of a Byzantine house. Some day, this house will slip quietly into the canal; now it merely leans in its eventual direction.

You might enter the garden via the gondola landing. Or, you might cross the footbridge, disappear into the narrow calle, and continue along to a doorway which opens directly into the garden. But if you are staying at the inexpensive Pensione Fioria, you might simply enter the garden from the Renaissance façade of the Pensione itself. Two steps lead up to this door.

It is late afternoon now and the wooden shutters of Venice are open wide. From beyond the garden come the chimes of

3

vague church bells, bursts of laughter, voices; from inside the Pensione comes a reedy but happy female voice singing a popular Italian song; and clearest of all, from over the wall comes the loud cry, "Gondola, Gondola!"

The setting sun has reserved some soft tones for the three people in the garden. One is SIGNORA FIORIA *who is sipping coffee and smoking. She wears sandals and a casual summer dress. She is rather tall, bony, dark and fortyish. Her physical attractiveness is more in her body than in her face; and, even more, in her manner. She is intelligent, perceptive, usually quiet (with her guests), has a sardonic humor, but we feel that she can blow up like a volcano. This feeling is probably influenced by the extremely uncomplicated sex she exudes without the slightest effort.*

The two others in the quiet garden are EDDIE *and* JUNE YAEGER, *a blonde and rather typically handsome young American couple. They are typical, too, in their manner and behavior, for, like so many, the* YAEGERS *try to be what they look and to conform to standard ideals. The crew-cut* EDDIE *is sprawled out in a chair, quite relaxed. Yet we feel his intensity. He is a painter, superior in Europe, inferior at home. He tries to be a high-spirited, casual, cheery, easygoing American. Naturally, he isn't (who is?) and the cracks show at times. He is slightly uneasy with his wife because his love for her is not pure. He has a deep need for her but they have never really talked or faced an important personal problem.*

JUNE *is extremely pretty, has a lovely body and adores her husband. Her concept of love, however, is romantic: she must be his complete life. She is sometimes insensitive out of ignorance and stubborn out of fear. Any unpleasantness, she rationalizes out of being. She is not very bright and although she knows this, she is not very bothered by it. Right now, for example, she is reading a big tome on Italian art—and paint-ing her fingernails.*

Both the YAEGERS, *like* FIORIA, *wear sandals.* EDDIE *has on light slacks and a white shirt,* JUNE *a light peasant dress. The peaceful silence lasts for a long moment. Then* EDDIE *reaches slowly to the table near him on which is a bottle and two glasses of Cinzano. He sips from one of the glasses. At this,* FIORIA *suddenly bellows:*

FIORIA

Giovanna!

EDDIE

If I were rich, I'd present Giovanna with an ice-cube ma-chine.

FIORIA

If I were rich, I'd present her with singing lessons. . . . Giovanna! (*For a moment, the singing stops. Then it re-sumes, though softer.* FIORIA *shrugs and sits back with a smile*) My husband used to say: if you are not going to fire her, the least you can do is strangle her.

JUNE

Honey, is Tiziano the same as Titian?

EDDIE

Yes.

JUNE

No wonder.

EDDIE

(*Laughs in the midst of a yawn and stretches*) I can learn to speak Italian, I can learn to do without showers, I cannot learn to drink without ice. I am warped.

JUNE

The kid feels good.

EDDIE

Si. Tomorrow, Signore, I start work.

FIORIA

Ah yes. Domani.

EDDIE

Not domani. Tomorrow.

JUNE

I hope so.

EDDIE

(*Correcting her previous pronunciation a trifle sharply*)
By the way, it's Tiziano.

FIORIA

Bene!

EDDIE

(*Rises—bows*)
Grazie, la mia professoressa.

FIORIA

Prego.
  (*He sits down again. They chuckle together. From over the wall, again the cry, "Gondola, Gondola!"*)

JUNE

If you ask me, he's not very ambitious.

EDDIE

You're talking to the wind. No one gets a rise out of me this evening.

JUNE

I meant the gondolier, honey.

FIORIA
(*After a moment*)
Why don't you think he is ambitious?

JUNE

There's nothing but pensiones around here. Why doesn't he park, or whatever they call it, over there—by the big hotels like the Danielli or the Europa?

FIORIA

He likes it here.

JUNE

Not very ambitious.

EDDIE
(*To* FIORIA)
You can't win.

'FIORIA

I think that gondolier does quite well here anyway. Don't you, Mr. Eddie?

EDDIE
(*Glances at her, then gets up, stretching*)
Oh, there's always an American who can be hooked.

(*Ruffles* JUNE's *hair*) Junie, you don't have to wade through all of Venetian Art tonight.

JUNE

It's lovely reading.

EDDIE

(*Imitating her pronunciation as he kisses her neck*)
Even Tiziano?

JUNE

(*Trapped by her wet fingernails*)
Turn the page for me, please, honey. (*He does*) Grazie tanto.

EDDIE

Prego, honey. (*His mouth slips down to hers. Then, to* FIORIA) Scusami, Signora.

FIORIA

I have pleasure in all kinds of lovemaking. (GIOVANNA, *a rather sloppy but nice-looking girl, shuffles out of the house in carpet slippers. She carries two small bowls: one with lemon peel, one with ice*) (FIORIA, *sarcastically*) Ah! Benvenuto, mia cara Giovanna.

(GIOVANNA *ignores this and hands* EDDIE *the ice, saying very carefully:*)

GIOVANNA

Lem-mon. (*Then, triumphantly, the lemon*) Ice!

EDDIE

I wish it were. Guarda, Giovanna: limone, lemon. Ghiaccio, ice.

GIOVANNA

To hell wit' English.

(*She goes into the house, singing a bit again.* EDDIE *sits down and fixes drinks for himself and* JUNE.)

JUNE

Believe you me, I know just how Giovanna feels. They can't even keep names the same. Tiziano for Titian; Venezia for Venice. You know, we were in Firenze one whole week before I found we were in Florence!

(*As they laugh, a woman appears on the footbridge, coming toward the garden. She is well in her thirties, blondish, plumpish, pleasantly attractive. She carries a large shoulder bag, a guidebook, a dictionary and one or two packages. Her name is* LEONA SAMISH. *She stops and calls out gaily:*)

LEONA

Buona sera!

FIORIA

(*Rises*)

Buona sera, Signorina! Come sta?

LEONA

Not so bene. I fell in a canal.

(*She grins as they laugh and disappears down the footbridge into the unseen calle behind the back wall of the garden.*)

EDDIE

I've just fallen in love.

JUNE

Her name is Leona Samish. I showed her where the bathroom was this morning.

EDDIE
(*Rises*)

Ah, an American.

LEONA

(*Entering the garden from the door in the rear*)
Wouldn't you just know?

> (*Close up*, LEONA *seems even more attractive. She wants so much to be liked and is by everyone almost at once. She is warm, she is generous, she is funny and bright. She is also lonely and, despite her many friends, always has been. But* LEONA's *pattern is to hide this, both from herself and the world, always with a joke and often with a drink. She is independent, she says, and almost believes it herself. There is something comforting and understanding and gay about* LEONA *that makes people glad to see her. Later, there is something else that makes them wonder why they do not cry.*)

FIORIA

You must be wet. (*Bellowing*) Giovanna!

LEONA

(*Dumping her parcels on the table*)
I'm semi-dried out now. It happened over an hour ago and anyway, I only fell in up to here. No, here.

EDDIE

Miss Samish, may I offer congratulations?

LEONA

It was nothing. A mere slip of the foot.

FIORIA

This is Mr. Eddie Yaeger.

EDDIE

You know my wife.

LEONA

Oh, sure. Hello, cookie.

JUNE

Hi.

LEONA

And you're the husband. Is there anyone on this continent who isn't spoken for? It's like Noah's Ark: everybody's in twos and I'm Noah.

EDDIE
(Bows)

Signora Noah.

LEONA

Signorina, unfortunately.

FIORIA

I am dying to know. How did you fall in?

LEONA

Feet first.

FIORIA

No. Details, please.
 (EDDIE *sits down.*)

LEONA

Well—you may not be aware of it, but you are looking at Leona Samish, Girl Tourist. I have to take a picture of everything. Even those bloody pigeons in front of San Marco. And that was a narrow escape, too. Anyway, this afternoon, I bought a goblet. Eighteenth-century Venetian glass, fellas. The wildest dark rose. And the only one left, damn it. I got it in a cute little shop—Di Rossi's.

FIORIA

Ah, yes. You should know Signor Di Rossi.

LEONA

I met him.

FIORIA
(*Smiling*)

Anh?

LEONA

I met him.

FIORIA
(*To* JUNE)

Silver-gray hair, prematurely gray.

EDDIE
(*Clapping his hands*)

Ladies, ladies. (*To* LEONA) You were saying . . . ?

LEONA

I wanted to get a picture of the shop where I bought the goblet, but a plain, simple picture wouldn't do. I never owned even a Brownie before this trip, but I have to have composition in the lousy picture. An authentic old Venetian church on one side and an authentic old Venetian lady on the other.

So—(*Acting it out now*)—I start backing up. I back up and up, and right in back of me was an authentic old Venetian canal. (*They laugh sadly; comes back to table*) I felt so foolish.

FIORIA

But it happens.

EDDIE

Who fished you out?

LEONA

I have an admirer. A little monster has been following me. The only male who has, I might add, and he's possibly a hot ten if he's a day. The minute I got to that gondola landing yesterday, there he was: "Lire, Signorina, lire."

FIORIA

He wears enormous blue jeans?

LEONA

And sings "Home on the Range."

FIORIA

Mauro.

LEONA

What?

EDDIE

That's his name: Mauro.

LEONA

Oh. Well, little Mauro fished me out. But I must say he was a lot more worried about my camera than about me.

EDDIE
(*Laughs*)

Have a drink.

JUNE

Honey, let her change first.

LEONA
(*Shaking out her skirt*)

Yeah. The charm of it all is beginning to seep through.

EDDIE
(*Rises*)

I'll get a glass for you meanwhile.

LEONA
(*Gathering up her packages*)

Don't anybody move. I'll be two seconds.

FIORIA

Giovanna can bring those up for you.

LEONA

We swimmers are a hardy lot. Where's my dictionary? Ah. (*Finding it, she kisses it*) I'd be speechless without it. Honest now, you'll all be here, won't you?

JUNE

Sure.

LEONA

I'll only be a minute. Don't go away. Oh, hello there!
(*She has started for the door into the Pensione just as
an elderly couple, the* MC ILHENNYS, *come out. They
both have white hair. He wears a wrinkled white suit,
shirt and tie, and a Panama hat which he whips off
at the sight of the ladies.* MRS. MC ILHENNY *wears a light
three-quarter coat over a print dress.* LEONA *rushes by
them.*)

MRS. MC ILHENNY

(*Sweetly, with a painful accent*)
Buona sera, Signore e Signor.

MR. MC ILHENNY

Oh, for Pete's sake, Edith!

FIORIA

Buona sera. You know Mr. and Mrs. Yaeger?

MRS. MC ILHENNY

We've seen each other, but we haven't had the pleasure.

FIORIA

Mr. and Mrs. McIl—I'm afraid I cannot say it.

MR. MC ILHENNY

McIlhenny.

JUNE

Hello.

EDDIE

Hello.
(FIORIA *sits down.*)

MR. MC ILHENNY
(*After a stiff pause*)
Well, the weather is nice here, anyway.

EDDIE
Excuse me. I have to get a glass.
(*He goes in.*)

JUNE
Don't you like Venice, Mr. McIlhenny?

MR. MC ILHENNY
(*To* FIORIA)
No disrespect intended, ma'am, but to me, it's just **Luna
Park** on water.

MRS. MC ILHENNY
Now, Lloyd. We've covered almost everything today, any-
way. Tomorrow, we're going to do the Lido, the Galeria
Academia and the Church of—what is it?

MR. MC ILHENNY
They're all alike to me.

JUNE
You should see the Biennale.

MRS. MC ILHENNY
Pardon?

JUNE
That's the big art exhibition at the Public Gardens.

MR. MC ILHENNY
If I have to look at one more painting, I'll yip.

FIORIA

Excuse me. Mrs. Yaeger's husband is an artist.

MRS. MC ILHENNY

How interesting!

MR. MC ILHENNY
(*To* JUNE)

No disrespect intended, ma'am. Truth is I don't understand pictures. And I've got bad feet for standing.

JUNE

I know how you feel. But when I fell in love with Eddie, I had to *get* to like pictures. So I looked and looked. Then one day, a wonderful thing happened: I knew what I was looking at! Kind of.

MRS. MC ILHENNY
(*Sitting*)

Would we have seen any of Mr. Yaeger's paintings? Someplace?

JUNE

Well, he had a one-man show in New York—that's sort of like getting a government contract, Mr. McIlhenny. (EDDIE *enters with two glasses*) And he sold a painting to the Museum of Modern Art, and one to the Toledo Museum and Peggy Guggenheim bought one.

EDDIE

Never mind the commercial, June.

MR. MC ILHENNY

You must be pretty successful.

EDDIE

That show was four years ago.

FIORIA

Are you going on to Firenze from here?
(MRS. MC ILHENNY *looks at June.*)

JUNE

That's Florence.

MRS. MC ILHENNY

Oh, yes, indeed! We're doing all of Italy: Florence, Rome,
Capri. And then off to Spain, Portugal, and home!

MR. MC ILHENNY

Flying home. Came over by boat.

EDDIE

You get around a bit.

MRS. MC ILHENNY

Dear me, yes!

MR. MC ILHENNY

We've been to Ireland, Scotland . . .

MRS. MC ILHENNY

The Edinburgh Festival was sweet.

MR. MC ILHENNY

England, London—France, Paris . . .

MRS. MC ILHENNY

(*Suspiciously*)

Well, Paris.

MR. MC ILHENNY

Belgium, Holland— (*Waits for* MRS. MC ILHENNY *but she beams without comment*) —Germany, Austria—

MRS. MC ILHENNY

Salzburg Festival. Dirndls!

MR. MC ILHENNY

—Switzerland, and here we are in Venice.

EDDIE

Some itinerary. How long you been at it?

MR. MC ILHENNY

Docked at Southampton 10:37 A.M. June fifteenth.

EDDIE

When are you flying from Portugal?

MR. MC ILHENNY

September ninth.

EDDIE

This year!

MRS. MC ILHENNY

I guess we have crowded things a bit.

MR. MC ILHENNY

Oh, no, dear. Our travel agency did a crackerjack job. Planned every step of the way. (*He has taken a paper from his pocket which he hands to* EDDIE) See? That was today.

EDDIE

(*Reading*)

"Eight A.M., breakfast; nine, Doge's Palace and Bridge of Sighs; 10 A.M.—San Marco Cathedral; 10:30-12:30—I.A." What's I.A.?

MR. MC ILHENNY

Independent activity. We have two hours of it every day.

EDDIE

(*Hands paper back*)

Oh.

MRS. MC ILHENNY

That's when I make him go shopping. It's our first trip abroad, you see. Mr. McIlhenny retired this year and we don't have any children, so—we decided to have our little fling while we still . . .

MR. MC ILHENNY

For Pete's sake, Edith.

EDDIE

(*Nicely*)

The trouble is everybody wants everybody else to have a good time their way.

MRS. MC ILHENNY

Yes. We've had a fine time. It's all been lovely, just lovely. (*Wistfully*) Not quite what we expected, perhaps . . .

JUNE

How do you mean?

MRS. MC ILHENNY

I don't know, really. I don't know what we expected, but . . . (*Brightly again*) Well, it's been lovely, just lovely. (*Starts for rear door.*)

EDDIE

Will you have a drink with us?

MR. MC ILHENNY

Well . . .

MRS. MC ILHENNY

No, dear. (*To* EDDIE) Thank you.

EDDIE

It's just Cinzano.
(LEONA, *in a fresh dress, comes out with a bottle in hand.*)

LEONA

How about a real drink with me and il Signor Gilbey: gin!

MRS. MC ILHENNY

We're on our way to dinner. We're going to Quadri's. Would you like to join us, Miss Samish?
(*From here the light begins to dim slowly to soft blue-purple evening.*)

LEONA

No, thanks. The book says that's a real elegant place.

EDDIE

And real expensive.
(*Hands her a drink.*)

LEONA

Thanks.

MRS. MC ILHENNY
(*Goes to her*)

Miss Samish, I meant to tell you. On the same side of the
piazza with Quadri's there's a big jewelry shop, and I'll bet
they have garnets.

LEONA

Oh, elegant. Garnets are my one passion. Well, garnets and
people. And Venice and the Pensione Fioria and an evening
like this. You're all so nice. (*The* MC ILHENNYS *start out*)
McIlhennys, don't go. Have a drink.

MR. MC ILHENNY

I'd like to, but this wop food has wrecked my digestion.

FIORIA

Then Quadri's is the perfect place. The cooking is **very**
light.

MR. MC ILHENNY

Good. Let's go, Edith.

MRS. MC ILHENNY

Well—arrivederci, all.

MR. MC ILHENNY

For Pete's sake, Edith.

MRS. MC ILHENNY
(*As they disappear from garden*)

Now Lloyd, you just let me be . . .
(*They are seen going over the bridge.*)

LEONA

(*Sitting*)

You think the Marshall Plan knows about him?

JUNE

He didn't know what he was saying, Signora.

FIORIA

He is not a sensitive man. He has no heart, not that much.
Italian food has ruined his miserable belly. He probably likes
French food!

LEONA

I must say I did.

FIORIA

But it's so refined! In Italy, you sit down to eat, and you
eat a meal. In Paris, you sit down, and what do you eat? A
sauce. And in America, this Mr. Mc—whatever it is—sits
down and what does he eat? Pills. You want me to get
excited about a man like that?

LEONA

Have a drink.

FIORIA

Grazie.

LEONA

Prego. (*Rises*) Hey, is that right?

EDDIE

Yes.

LEONA

It's used for so many things, I figure when in doubt, say
"prego."

EDDIE

Junie, we ought to be getting a move on.

JUNE

I'm so lazy.

LEONA

Ah, have a drink. It's good gin, cookie.

EDDIE

No, thanks.

LEONA

Prego? Pretty prego?

EDDIE

We're late for dinner. (JUNE *starts to gather her things.*
EDDIE *takes the Cinzano. To* JUNE) I'll carry that, hon. (*To*
LEONA) Give us a rain check.

LEONA

Sure. (*The* YAEGERS *go into the house a moment, then:*)
Sure you won't have one?

FIORIA

No, no, grazie.

LEONA

I thought in a pensione, everyone had meals in.

FIORIA

Most prefer demi-pension so they can have either lunch or
dinner out. Usually dinner.

LEONA

Well—that leaves us. Or does it? I guess it doesn't.

FIORIA

I am dining with an old friend.

LEONA

Signor Di Rossi?

FIORIA

No. Faustino is his name. He is in the government. For fifteen years, he has been in our government.

LEONA

All your governments?

FIORIA

(*Laughs*)

He is very sophisticated. Why did you ask if it was Di Rossi?

LEONA

You said you knew him.

FIORIA

I see him here and there.

LEONA

I saw him in the piazza last night, in front of Florian's. I didn't know who he was then, but you can't miss that silver hair. Look, if you have to go, Signora, please do. I enjoy being alone.

FIORIA

Are you a writer?

LEONA

Just a fancy secretary, really.

FIORIA

Then why do you like to be alone? I hate it!

LEONA

I'm the independent type. Always have been. Got time for a short one?

FIORIA

Yes, but I don't want it, thank you.

LEONA

Mayhap I can persuade myself. (*Raising the bottle*) Prego? (*Pouring*) Grazie. This is a nice place. There are two people in the States I wish were here. A darling couple, but they can't move two feet without me. (*Raising her glass*) Luck. They're rather like the Yaegers, except Mac and Franny are older. Not older than me, older than the Yaegers. *Nobody's* older than me.

FIORIA

I am. And in Italy, age is an asset.
(*Off in the city, bells chime.*)

LEONA

If it is, I'm loaded. You know, I took this vacation to get away and be on my own. And what happens first night out on the boat? Up pops a honeymoon couple. Helpless kids, but sweet. We had a ball in Paris. What a city!

FIORIA

Yes.

LEONA

You don't have to go yet, do you?

FIORIA
(*Sits*)

No.

LEONA

Everything everybody ever said, wrote or sang about Paris is true. Except you shouldn't be allowed there unless you're in love. Paris is just laid out for it.

FIORIA

So is Venice.

LEONA

So is any place, if you have it. Paris is beautiful except— I don't know. I don't really know what I expected. On the train coming here, I met another American girl. In America, Signora, every female under fifty is a girl.

FIORIA

And after fifty?

LEONA

Who cares? This girl on the train was waiting.

FIORIA

For what?

LEONA

She came to Europe to find something. It was way back in the back of her mind: past seeing places and getting some culture—that was up front, here. (*Touches her forehead*) Buying perfume cheap was about here, and letting loose for once was about here. But way *way* back was the something she was waiting for.

FIORIA

What?

LEONA

A wonderful mystical magical miracle.

FIORIA

No! To do what?

LEONA

Beats me. I guess to find her whatever it was she'd been missing all her life. The bargains some people expect on a hot six-week vacation! Now you do have to go.

FIORIA

Would you care to come with me?

LEONA

Oh, no. Thank you, no.

FIORIA

When in Italy, you should meet Italians.

LEONA

Two's company . . .

FIORIA

Oh, Miss Samish! Signor Faustino and I are, oh, for several years now, we have been—ahh—(*Waves her hands, as though to pluck the word from the air*)—unexcited.

LEONA

By me, you're a twosome. (*Shaking her head*) Grazie tanto.

FIORIA

Prego.
(*They laugh.*)

LEONA

Va bene! Oh, there's no holding me! (FIORIA *starts toward house, stops and turns back.* LEONA *goes to her*) Don't worry, Signora. I do fine on my own. Last night, I had dinner with the McIlhennys. I feel sad for them: the "big fling" they're having. They went to bed right after dinner but I had coffee in San Marco and listened to that lovely band concert.

FIORIA

The concerts are every next night.

LEONA

Oh. Maybe I'll take a gondola after dinner.

FIORIA

Oh, don't take a gondola alone at night. Wait.

LEONA

O.K. I mean va bene. Have a good time.

FIORIA

Thank you. (*Stops on her way into the house*) Would you like dinner out here?

LEONA

Yes, I would, if it isn't too much bother for Giovanna.

FIORIA

None at all. Just don't let her rush you.

LEONA

Giovanna?

FIORIA

After sunset, she rushes around like an American. She has a friend: Alfredo. All day long, she is only recuperating from the night before.

LEONA

I should be so sick.

FIORIA

And I! Buona sera.

LEONA

Buona sera. (FIORIA *enters the Pensione. The dusk is light purple now.* LEONA *sits at table and takes a sip of her drink. Then she just sits. From the right, far-off music is heard, a lovely Italian tune. It has a lonely sound and, after a moment,* LEONA *gets up and wanders about the garden, looking up at the buildings, seeming a little lost. She sees something, perhaps up in the tree, perhaps in the shadows on the rear wall— puts her drink on table and goes to rear door*) Here, kitty, kitty, kitty. Pretty little baby. Here, kitty, kitty. Please . . . How do you say it in Italian? Ssspsspsspsspssss. (*But the unseen cat goes*) Ah, kitty . . . (*She straightens up and listens to the music again. From over the canal wall comes the cry, softer now: "Gondola, Gondola!"* LEONA *moves toward the wall, then abruptly, lights go on in the garden—gay, gently colored bulbs strung through the arbor and the tree. She whirls around. A moment, and* GIOVANNA *comes out carrying a tray and collects the empty glasses*) Giovanna. Lei a . . .
(*She points to the lights.*)

GIOVANNA

Si, si. Molto bella, ah?

LEONA

Oh, molto bella.

GIOVANNA
(*Making conversation*)
Venezia è molto bella.

LEONA

Si. Venezia è molto bella.

GIOVANNA

Si.

LEONA

Alfredo è molto bella.

(GIOVANNA *stares at her, then bursts into laughter and runs into the house. Alone again with the music,* LEONA *sits at table. She sips her drink, gets her voluminous bag, rummages around and comes up with cigarettes, postcards and a pen. She sips her drink and starts to write:*)

Dearest Mac and Franny: Venice is as unbelievable as a musical comedy. How I wish you both were—(*Stops, puts the pen down and sits for a long, lonely moment. Even the music has stopped. Then:*)—you both were here because this time, we'd be a quartet. Mio amico has silver-gray hair . . . (*She stops again and looks in the direction of the Pensione. A moment, then* JUNE *comes out. She is now wearing high-heeled sandals and a thin sweater over her dress*) Cookie, you're a very pretty girl.

JUNE
(On step)

I know but I'm not interesting looking. Like the women in paintings. (*Goes to her*) You are.

LEONA
(Rises, turns away)

Oh, go on.

JUNE

You are! (LEONA *turns away*) What's the matter?

LEONA
(Too touched by this)

Niente. (*Turns back, smiling*) Say, when your fella's busy with his pallette, how about you showing me the town? Maybe we could go swimming?

JUNE

Sure!

EDDIE

(*Breezing on in a light jacket now and loafers and socks*)
Pronto, Signora Yaeger?

JUNE
(*Pokes him*)
I've been pronto for ten minutes.

EDDIE
(*Slapping her on the fanny*)
I told you that was a great color for you. (*To* LEONA) We
are off. Off to a real Venetian pizzeria: Harry's Bar.

LEONA

The book says that's a Must.

EDDIE

You don't Must, but you will. (*He has been fumbling for
a match for his cigarette;* LEONA *gives him one*) Thanks.
Excuse us?

LEONA

Sure. Have fun.

JUNE

See you.
(*She leaves the garden with* EDDIE.)

LEONA

Right. (*They are almost over the footbridge when she calls:*)
Say! Why don't I get it over with and give Harry his big
break tonight? (*Pause*) Would it be all right if I walked
along with you?

EDDIE

(*On the bridge*)

. . . Sure.

LEONA

(*Runs to her bag, sweeps the things in*)

I always buy my guides a drink.

EDDIE

We're meeting some friends.

LEONA

Oh. Well, can I buy them a drink, too? Or are there too many?

JUNE

Just another couple, but . . .

LEONA

It would be awkward.

EDDIE

We're going on to dinner together from Harry's.

LEONA

Oh, sure. (*Puts her bag down*) I guess I'll just have to give you another rain check, that's all.

EDDIE

We'll take it.

JUNE

Good night.

LEONA

Buona sera. Or do you say—what is it?—ciao.

EDDIE

Well, you really say "ciao" to family and very close friends. Otherwise, buona sera. Or—arrivederci.

LEONA

Oh. Arrivederci, Signor. Arrivederci, Signora.

JUNE

Arrivederci.

EDDIE
(Nicely)

Arrivederci.

(He takes JUNE'S *arm and they go.* LEONA *watches them leave, then slowly walks back to the table. She stuffs a postcard or two left lying there into her bag, then stands. She picks up her glass, looks at it, then, with a wry smile, raises it and says:)*

LEONA

Ciao, honey.

(She finishes the drink as GIOVANNA *enters with a tray on which is* LEONA'S *dinner. She puts the tray on the table as from the house comes a thin, scratchy phonograph record of an Italian singing some tune.)*

GIOVANNA

Buona notte, Signorina.

LEONA

Buona notte, Giovanna.

(GIOVANNA goes. LEONA *slowly sits and takes the napkin from the tray and carefully spreads it on her lap. She arranges the dishes a bit, then reaches into her bag for her guidebook. She opens it, props it against the glass so she can read as she slowly begins her lonely dinner. From the canal comes the soft cry, "Gondola! Gondola!" Someone laughs.)*

Curtain

ACT ONE

Scene II

*Early afternoon heat. All the shutters in Venice are closed.
Even the doorway to the Pensione has slatted wooden doors
to bar the sun. The* YAEGERS *are stretched out, lazily sunning
in canvas deck chairs.*

*On a table against left wall, is an empty beer bottle; in a
pail of ice is another (but full) bottle covered with a towel.
Both* JUNE *and* EDDIE *have a glass of beer carefully placed in
the shadows cast by their own chairs. There is a footstool
below* JUNE'S *chair. There is a table near center with a glass
on it.*

*JUNE is lying still and serene, her face tilted to the sun. By
her side is a pair of sunglasses, a bottle of suntan oil and the
big art book.* EDDIE *is on his back. He kicks at a fly. The sun
pours down in the silence. He tries to swat the fly but only
smacks himself loudly. He rolls over irritably.*

EDDIE

We ought to be locked in a madhouse. You don't catch
any Italians cremating themselves to look healthy! (*Shifts his
position, lies still, then reaches for his beer but knocks the
glass over*) Damnation! (*The beer has spilled. He gets up
and goes to the table. En route, he stubs his toe*) Judas Priest!
(JUNE *opens her eyes*) These damn slobby Italians can't put
down a level floor! (JUNE *closes her eyes and erases the smile
as he looks at her suspiciously. At the same time, the canal
wall door opens and a head peers out. Then the thin, bony
frame of a twelve-year-old Italian boy in a slightly torn T-shirt
and faded, oversize blue jeans held up by rope appears from
canal door.* EDDIE *limps over to the table and in taking the*

35

beer bottle from the pail, cracks his shin against a bench. He roars:) God in heaven! (JUNE *laughs out loud. He whirls on her*) Very funny. Crack your shin and let me laugh! (*She cannot stop and the boy, watching, begins to guffaw.* EDDIE *whips around and yells:*) You little son of a bitch! (*Holding the bottle and opener, he takes a threatening step to the kid*) Fuori dai piedi! Via! (*The kid ducks out the canal wall door. Furiously,* EDDIE *opens the beer—and foam shoots out all over him. A split moment of dead silence. He looks at* JUNE—*then breaks up, and they both howl. He dries himself with the towel*) At least, it's cold. Want some more?

JUNE

Please. Was Mauro swimming in the canal again?

EDDIE
(*Filling his own glass now*)
No. Probably taking his siesta in an empty gondola. Terrible how Italian children learn all those four-letter words.

JUNE

Honey, you're hungover.

EDDIE
(*Going back to his chair*)
It's why I'm hungover.

JUNE
(*Eyes shut, sunbathing*)
You drank too much last night.

EDDIE
(*His eyes shut, too; his voice a sun-heavy monotone:*)
Why oh why oh why. (*Trying a different rhythm:*) Oh why oh why oh why oh . . . Because I was finally, finally going to start work today. I stink.

JUNE

You do not.

EDDIE

Now let's have an argument whether or not I stink.

JUNE

No, no. You stink. (EDDIE *sips beer. Pause. They sunbathe*) It's all the fault of that man in New York that said the paintings you did since the show would make nice Christmas cards.

EDDIE

Unlike the rest of us, Mr. Sonnabend is not alone.

JUNE

I'll bet there's a lot of money in Christmas cards. Well, they're very popular! What if you paint them one time and museum pieces the next? The important thing is to paint. . . . Isn't it, honey?

EDDIE

Yes.

JUNE

Well?

EDDIE

(*Sits up*)

June, it's hard. It's doubly hard when you hit it the first time and have to compete with yourself. And I think: maybe I *should* give up. Maybe all I *am* good for is Christmas cards. But June, I don't want to give up just yet.

JUNE

Isn't that silly? I thought the trouble was all because of me.

EDDIE

You? No.

JUNE
(*Lies back*)

That's a relief!

EDDIE
(*Leans back*)

Sometimes I think language is a means of excommunication.

JUNE

Please don't say things I don't understand.

EDDIE

I'm sorry.

JUNE

We can talk: I've learned a lot. You just won't try. (*Sits up*)
Ask me about Carpaccio.

EDDIE
(*Sits up*)

June, I know you try and I appreciate it. It breaks me all
up inside.

JUNE

You don't have to break up. Just ask me about Carpaccio.

EDDIE

Honey, talking isn't an exam.

JUNE
(*Leans back*)

O.K., I'm dumb. So let's don't talk and *I* can at least sunbathe out the lines.

EDDIE

I'm sorry.
(*Lies back, closes his eyes.*)

JUNE
(*After a moment*)

There was a very interesting article in the paper the other day about that strike in Turin. I think those men are silly. They'll never get their jobs back. (*Pause*) Did you read it?

EDDIE

The strike was settled yesterday.

JUNE

. . . I guess they got their jobs back.

EDDIE

Yes.

JUNE
(*After a silence, touches his hand*)

Honey, it's been better since we've been in Venice.

EDDIE

I haven't finished one thing.

JUNE

I meant Us.

EDDIE

Oh.

JUNE

I'm sorry.

EDDIE

No. Honey, I wish that were better.

JUNE

Eddie, I love you. It doesn't matter a hoot to me if you can't paint like you used to. I don't care if you paint at all. All I want is for you to be happy and to love me.

EDDIE

I do.

JUNE

Tell me.

EDDIE

I love you.

JUNE

You're *in* love with me.

EDDIE

June . . . (*Then*) I'm *in* love with you.

JUNE

Honey, we'll be fine. It's just your hangover.

EDDIE
(*Chanting tunelessly*)

Oh, honey, we'll be fine, indeed we'll be fine, oh honey, we'll be fine indeed.

(JUNE *waves her hand at him, blindly. He catches her hand and holds it. They lie there quiet, peaceful, their eyes closed to the sun and themselves.*)

(*In the silence,* LEONA *enters the garden from the rear door with all her tourist paraphernalia and a package identical to one she had the day before. When she sees the* YAEGERS, *she stops and hesitates wistfully. Then she starts to walk by them on tiptoe but* EDDIE *opens his eyes.*)

LEONA

I thought you had baked yourselves to sleep. (JUNE *opens her eyes*) Hi.

JUNE
(Sitting up)

Hi.

(EDDIE *sits up. Brief, awkward pause.*)

LEONA

Say, I haven't gotten a picture of you two yet.

EDDIE

Oh, no!

LEONA
(Putting package and bag on table)

Be a sport. I could use some cheesecake between churches.

JUNE

Come on, honey.

EDDIE
(As LEONA *prepares her camera)*

I hate this.

JUNE

I love it.

EDDIE
(Grinning)

Peacock.

JUNE

Uh-huh.

LEONA

You'll have to get close. I have small eyes.

(*As they get ready,* MAURO *sticks his head out the canal
door again, then comes into the garden to watch.*)

EDDIE
(*To* LEONA)

About last night . . .

LEONA

Forget it.

EDDIE

No. You see, we . . .

MAURO
(*To* LEONA, *who is focusing her camera*)

Hey, lady, wanna buy real good Swiss watch? Ten dollar.

LEONA

Not this minute.

MAURO

You crazy? It got works inside. (*Holding the watch out to* EDDIE) Look! Tell her!

LEONA

Hold it! (*Snaps picture*) Grazie.

MAURO
(*Goes to her*)

You take my picture?

LEONA

Yes.

MAURO
(*Plaintively, with outstretched hand*)

Lire, Signorina.

LEONA

You know, I think that's all the Italian the kid knows. (*To* MAURO) Listen, Signor Lira, you were supposed to take me to the Galeria Academia this morning, remember?

MAURO
(*Scratching his head*)
This morning?

LEONA
Si. This morning. I got lost. Where were you?

MAURO
Tsk tsk tsk. I have business.

LEONA
Is that so?

MAURO
(*Importantly*)
I work for my friend, de gondolier. Every customer I bring, he pay me. Why you no wanna buy good Swiss watch?

LEONA
I have a watch.

MAURO
Only ten dollar. Come on. What da hell.

EDDIE
Mauro, va via. (*The kid retreats. To* LEONA *as she puts camera on table*) I was going to say . . . Oh, excuse me. Beer?

LEONA
Beer gives me a cardboard mouth.

JUNE
(*Holding out her glass*)
Have a sip. It's cool, anyway.

LEONA
Well, that's more than I am.
(*She drinks, returns glass.*)

MAURO

(*To* LEONA)

Lady, wanna buy Parker 51 Pen? (*Holding one out*) 2,000 lire.

LEONA

No, thanks.

EDDIE

Cigarette? (*She takes one*) For the last five minutes, I've been trying to—well . . .

MAURO

Lady, special price for you: 1500 lire.

EDDIE

Mauro! (*The kid scampers. To* LEONA) What I started to say was . . . (*Lights her cigarette*) Oh, hell. I'm trying to find a way of apologizing for last night that won't embarrass either of us.

LEONA

That does it very nicely, cookie.

EDDIE

We were kind of trapped. We're sorry and **we** wanted you to know.

LEONA

Well—grazie tanto *and* prego.

EDDIE

Prego to you.

JUNE

You were up early this morning 'cause we looked.

LEONA

Girl Tourist. (*Holding up her guidebook*) I'm attempting to zip through the six-day tour in three and a half.

EDDIE

Why the rush?

LEONA

I've got to be back in the salt mines around Labor Day, and I should see Rome.

EDDIE

Why?

JUNE

Maybe there's someone in Rome she wants to see.

LEONA

It's a big city, there should be. (*Wryly as she sits on footstool*) Ah me. When I was a kid, I used to wish on the moon.

JUNE

I still do.

LEONA

Any luck?

JUNE
(*Looks at* EDDIE)

Uh-huh.

LEONA

I'm thinking of giving the stars my business.

MAURO

Lady, you got any brothers and sisters?

LEONA

Three, cookie.

MAURO

You very lucky. For t'ree brudders and sisters, I got t'ree
Parker 51 Pens. (*Holds them up*) Presents. Souvenir of Italy!

LEONA

No, Mauro.

MAURO

Special for you . . .

LEONA

No.

MAURO

Come on. What da hell?

LEONA

How do you say No in Italian?

EDDIE

Watch.
(*Turns to* MAURO *who immediately backs away.*)

MAURO

O.K., O.K., I only want to give her present. You so pretty
and nice, here, lady.
(*Puts pen in her hand.*)

LEONA
(*Touched*)

Why, Mauro!

MAURO

You like?

LEONA

Very much.

MAURO

One thousand lire, Signorina?
(LEONA *shoves the pen back into his outstretched hand and* EDDIE *advances on him.*)

EDDIE

O.K., regazzo.
(*The kid scampers over to the canal door.*)

LEONA

He'll hook me yet. What's more, he knows it. (*Waves at the little figure*) Arrivederci, Mauro.

EDDIE

(*Putting on his shirt*)
Tan or no tan, I quit.

LEONA

(*Rises, indicating* MAURO)
He's the one shop in all Venice that doesn't close in the afternoon. (*To the mournful-looking boy*) Nothing today. (*A step toward him*) Cookie, it's so hot. Close up for a few hours. I'll be around. (*He just stares*) Ah, Mauro . . .

MAURO

You no buy nutting now?

LEONA

No.

MAURO

You no give me lira?

LEONA

I gave you yesterday.

MAURO

Then give me cigarette.
(EDDIE *laughs.*)

LEONA

You're too little to smoke.

MAURO

But I smoke!

LEONA

Not with my help.

MAURO

Come on. One cigarette. What da hell.

LEONA

(*Laughs and reaches in her bag*)
You know a sucker when you see one. Here. (*He reaches greedily for the cigarette*) Easy does it.

MAURO

Grazie.

LEONA

Prego.

MAURO

You O.K., lady. (*Grinning slyly to* JUNE *and* EDDIE) So long, cookies.
(*Pushes open the door and goes.*)

EDDIE

(*Folding his chair*)
Coming up, June?

JUNE

Do you want me to?

EDDIE

(Joking to cover his annoyance as he puts chair against wall)
Oh, for Pete's sake, Edith.

JUNE

I thought maybe you wanted to be alone to think.

EDDIE

If I did, I would've said so. *(To* LEONA*)* See you later.

LEONA

You bet.
(He goes into the Pensione.)

JUNE

He's a little hungover, that's all that was.

LEONA

Have a big time last night?

JUNE

(Putting on a robe and gathering up her things; folds her chair and puts it alongside of EDDIE's*)*
No. Those friends we were with—well—she's a very rich American who collects art. The husband is kind of an Italian count. Eddie's here on a fellowship. The Contessa buys us drinks and dinner, and maybe when Eddie does a painting, she'll buy it. Oh, she's very nice. But she kind of doesn't like unattached women around. *(Embarrassed, she quickly picks up art book and sees* LEONA's *package)* What'd you buy?

LEONA

(Getting package)
A mate for that Venetian glass goblet I told you I got yesterday.

JUNE

At Di Rossi's?

LEONA

(Unwrapping the goblet)

Yes.

JUNE

Wasn't he nice to find another one!

LEONA

He wasn't there. I saw him in the Piazza last night, though.
We nodded. (JUNE *is waiting for more.* LEONA *smiles*) That's
all.

JUNE

Oh.

*(Over the little stone footbridge comes a man wearing
a pale-blue shirt and light trousers. A jacket dangles
from one shoulder. He looks over into the garden at
the two women who do not see him. Forty-odd, he has
slightly tired good looks made striking by prematurely
silver-gray hair. This, of course, is* DI ROSSI, *a man most
women are attracted to and whom most men like. He
is invariably at ease, and although he is a worldly man,
his knowledge is a product of experience and his senses
rather than of his mind and thought. He is so very
charming, so direct, so simple (like a child) that it is
difficult to believe he might not always tell the precise
truth. At any rate, since he always believes it is the
truth when he is saying it and since there is so much
truth in what he does say, does it matter? Actually, it
shouldn't, if only because* RENATO DI ROSSI *is very eager
to accept almost anyone and almost any moment. . . .
A moment, then he continues across the bridge and*

disappears into the calle behind the garden. During this, LEONA *has unwrapped the goblet and* JUNE *takes it, exclaiming:*)

JUNE

Isn't it dreamy!

LEONA

Eighteenth century.

JUNE

Were they terribly expensive?

LEONA

1600 lira each.

JUNE

My! How much is that in money?

LEONA

I'm still with French francs. Under three bucks, anyway. (JUNE *sighs as she hands it back*) Cookie, it was very sweet of you to explain about last night.

JUNE

Oh . . .

LEONA

It was. What're you going to be doing later on?

JUNE

Depends on Eddie. We might go swimming over the Lido.

LEONA

Gee, I have one of those French bathing suits.

JUNE

Oh. Well, if we decide to go, we'll knock on your door.

LEONA

(*A step toward her*)

Would you? When would that be?

JUNE

In an hour or so.

LEONA

You won't forget?

JUNE

No.

LEONA

If I'm not in my room, I'll be down here.

JUNE

(*At the door*)

O.K.

LEONA

If by any chance, I go out on one of my tours, I'll leave a note saying where I am.

JUNE

All right.

(*Enters the house.*)

(DI ROSSI *now enters the garden.*)

LEONA

(*Hurrying back to the table with the goblet*)

I'd better hold onto that box so I can pack this. I'll only be a . . .

(*But the door has closed after* JUNE. LEONA *stands, unaware of* DI ROSSI *who mops his brow with a handkerchief. As she slowly begins to re-wrap the goblet, he comes up with a smile.*)

DI ROSSI

(*A soft but marked accent*)

Good afternoon.

LEONA
(*Turns, startled*)
Oh . . . Hello, there.

DI ROSSI
Hello.

LEONA
You played hooky this morning.

DI ROSSI
I beg your pardon?

LEONA
I bought this at your shop. Didn't the boy tell you?

DI ROSSI
Yes.

LEONA
He was very kind. And very cute.

DI ROSSI
He is my niece.

LEONA
(*Laughs*)
Your nephew.

DI ROSSI
(*Laughs*)
Oh, yes, nephew, nephew! Just when I think I speak English like a trooper, something happens. Anyway, he is the son of my eldest sister.

LEONA
Bravo!

DI ROSSI

Grazie.

LEONA

Prego. And that about concludes my entire performance in Italiano.

(*She puts goblet back in box. He moves to table.*)

DI ROSSI

Is this beer?

LEONA

Help yourself. It isn't mine.

DI ROSSI
(*Smiles*)

Thank you.

LEONA

. . . Shall I call someone for you?

DI ROSSI

Who?

LEONA

I don't know. Signora Fioria?

DI ROSSI

I scarcely know her.
(*Sips beer.*)

LEONA

Oh.

DI ROSSI

Do you want to call someone?

LEONA

No.

DI ROSSI
(*Puts glass down*)

I came to see you.

LEONA

Oh. (*Sits*) Oh! You found some more of those glasses.

DI ROSSI

Unfortunately, no. But perhaps there is something else I might find for you?

LEONA

You don't happen to know a good black market in money?

DI ROSSI

The best. And very legitimate. (LEONA *laughs*) But that's easy. Give me something difficult.

LEONA

Why?

DI ROSSI

So I can do it for you.

LEONA

. . . I've been trying to find some garnets.

DI ROSSI

Garnet?

LEONA

They're jewelry. Dark red stones.

DI ROSSI

Ah. Rubies.

LEONA

Not on my salary. Garnets—garnets.

DI ROSSI

(*Sadly*)

I'm sorry. No.

LEONA

Where's my book? (*Getting it and thumbing through*) Not that there's anything useful in here. "At the restaurant . . . The Motor Accident . . . The Shipwreck . . . At the Hospital." (*Plunks it down. Rises, goes to him*) Garnets. They're not expensive. Do you know topaze?

DI ROSSI

Si.

LEONA

Garnets are a semi-precious stone like that. But red and small . . .

DI ROSSI

(*Thinks a moment, then:*)

Ah, granate!

LEONA

(*Shaking his hand*)

We did it!

DI ROSSI

Yes! . . . There are not many garnet in Venice any more. But we will look.

LEONA

Don't go to any trouble.

DI ROSSI

For you, it is not trouble. (*Pause. Mopping his brow*) You don't mind the heat.

LEONA

Signor Di Rossi, why did you come to see me?

DI ROSSI
(Smiles)

It is only natural. After all, you are not going to keep buying glasses every day.

LEONA

No.

DI ROSSI

So—I came.

LEONA

But why?

DI ROSSI

Why? You knew I would.

LEONA

I did not!

DI ROSSI

Maybe it's my English.

LEONA

Maybe it's mine.
(Turns away.)

DI ROSSI
(Goes to her)

Listen. Two nights ago, I am in Piazza San Marco. You are in Piazza San Marco. We look. Next day, you are in my shop. We talk about glasses, we talk about Venice. You like Venice? I like Venice.

LEONA

Molto bella.

DI ROSSI

Si, molto bella. I understand your jokes. Ecco. We talk about Venice, glasses, but we are not speaking about them, are we? No. So, last night, I am in Piazza San Marco again, you are in Piazza San Marco again.

LEONA

Half of Venice is in Piazza San Marco again!

DI ROSSI

But half of Venice is not in my shop this morning or I would be a rich man!

LEONA

I wanted another glass.

DI ROSSI

And that's all?

LEONA

That's all!

DI ROSSI

There are shops all over Venice. Did you look in any of them for your glass?

LEONA

No.

DI ROSSI

Ah!

LEONA

But you said you would try to find one for me!

DI ROSSI

And that is why you came back.

LEONA

Yes!

DI ROSSI

No other reason?

LEONA
(Shaking)

I don't know what your experience has been with American tourists . . .
(She turns away.)

DI ROSSI

My experience has been that tourists have more experience than I! *(He mops his brow)* It's very hot. Can't we sit down?

LEONA
(Half-angry, half-crying)

No!
(Turns away.)

DI ROSSI

I have offended you. *(She shakes her head)* You are sorry I am here.

LEONA

No.

DI ROSSI
(A smile)

Then you are glad.

LEONA
(Turning to him)

All this may be silly to you, but—I'm not an Italian. I'm an American.

DI ROSSI

I thought everything happened so fast in America.

LEONA

Not this sort of thing. Not to me.
(She turns away.)

DI ROSSI

I *have* offended you.

LEONA

(*Turns back*)

Signor, I'm not a child. But I don't understand.

DI ROSSI

What?

LEONA

Why should you want to see me?

DI ROSSI

Because when we spoke yesterday, I knew you were sim-patica. You know what that means?

LEONA

Yes: like a sister to me.

DI ROSSI

I have four sisters and I am not looking for another. (*Smiles*) Oh—you were making a joke. You make many jokes but inside, I think you cry. (*Touched, she turns away and sits, her back to him*) That is nice; that is why you are simpatica. (*A pause. He draws up a chair behind her. Very quietly:*) I came here to ask if you would do me the honor of seeing me this evening. I would like to take you to dinner but I cannot. Our family is very large. At a nice restaurant, I could not even pay for myself. But, if you would like, we could have coffee together in the Piazza. There is the concert tonight. All Puccini. Do you like Puccini?

LEONA

Yes.

DI ROSSI

Would you have coffee with me?

LEONA

. . . I'd like a cigarette.
(*Turns around.*)

DI ROSSI

I have only Italian cigarettes.

LEONA

I have some. (*During the following, she gets one from her bag which* DI ROSSI *lights for her*) Signor, I'm afraid you've made a small mistake.

DI ROSSI

Why?

LEONA

. . . When I was about your nephew's age, I had three children to bring up.

DI ROSSI

Three?

LEONA

Yes.

DI ROSSI

It is Miss Samish?

LEONA

It always has been.

DI ROSSI

Ah, I see. Well . . . (*Smiles*) I admire you. It is not a sin in Italy, you know.

LEONA

A sin?

DI ROSSI

Not if the children are baptized. Yours were, of course?

LEONA

Oh no, look . . .

DI ROSSI

Perhaps you don't believe in baptism. (*Grins*) Anyway,
I am not the Pope.

LEONA

They weren't my children. They're my two brothers and
my sister.

DI ROSSI

But . . .

LEONA

You decided they were mine.

DI ROSSI

You seemed to have something to tell me, so naturally . . .

LEONA

(*Rises and he gets up*)

"Naturally" seems to mean only one thing in Italy. . . .
My father died when I was sixteen. He didn't leave anything
because he never had anything. Six months after, my mother
died. I had to bring up the kids. . . . Do you understand?

DI ROSSI

Some words here and there I may miss. But I understand.
You say you are not rich and if that is why I am here, I am
making an error. You do not know me very well yet,
Signorina, so you are not insulting me. But yourself you know.
Don't you?

LEONA

Very well.

DI ROSSI

(*Gently*)

Then why do you insult yourself?

LEONA

(*Shaking her head*)

You come to see me . . .

DI ROSSI

You cannot understand why.

LEONA

No.

DI ROSSI

(*Goes to her*)

Because you attract me. Why? Because you do. Why? I do not know. (*Smiles*) You Americans are even more suspicious than the French. Listen: we saw each other, we liked each other. This is so nice, how can it be wrong? (*Smiles*) You are very young, Miss Samish.

(*Through the rear door, the* MC ILHENNYS *enter the garden laden with packages.*)

MRS. MC ILHENNY

Buon giorno, Signorina Samish. We've been shopping!

MR. MC ILHENNY

Let her guess, Edith.

LEONA

This is Signor Di Rossi. Mr. and Mrs. McIlhenny.

MRS. MC ILHENNY

Come sta, Signor?

DI ROSSI

Bene, grazie. E Lei?

MRS. MC ILHENNY

Bene, grazie.

DI ROSSI

Non fa troppo caldo per Lei, Signora?

MRS. MC ILHENNY

Oh, dear!

MR. MC ILHENNY
(*Laughs*)

Serves you right.

LEONA

What'd you buy?

MRS. MC ILHENNY
(*Goes to her*)

Glass, glass and more glass.

MR. MC ILHENNY
(*Rather proudly*)

She even sent home a chandelier.

MRS. MC ILHENNY

We found a place behind San Marco Cathedral—oh, I've got
to show you!
(*Starts to undo a package as she puts it on table.*)

MR. MC ILHENNY

Now, Edith . . .

MRS. MC ILHENNY

But they're so pretty, Lloyd.

LEONA

What are they?

MRS. MC ILHENNY

Venetian glass.

LEONA

Don't bother to unwrap them.

MRS. MC ILHENNY

I must show just one. And you've got to go to this place.
They have a blast furnace, and you sit right there and watch

them put stuff on long poles and presto, chango! Glass! And such colors, you have no—there! Isn't that exquisite?

(What she has unwrapped is a goblet exactly like the one LEONA *has.)*

LEONA

Stunning. Oddly enough, I was looking for one just like it.

MRS. MC ILHENNY

Oh, they're only too happy to make them for you. I bought half a dozen.

DI ROSSI

If I may ask, how much did you pay?

MR. MC ILHENNY

Too much.

MRS. MC ILHENNY

(Returning the goblet to the box)

Lloyd, you know I did extremely well. They wanted 2500 lira apiece but you never give them what they want. Beat them down every—oh! I'm terribly sorry.

DI ROSSI

No, no. Italians love to bargain. What did you pay finally?

MRS. MC ILHENNY

2100 apiece. That's a fair price, isn't it?

LEONA

It's fair.

MR. MC ILHENNY

Edith, we have a lot of packing to do.

MRS. MC ILHENNY

We! He can't even pack his own toothbrush. *(To* DI ROSSI *who has helped her with her packages)* Why, Grazie!

DI ROSSI

Prego.

MR. MC ILHENNY

Nice to have met you, Mr. Di Rossi.

DI ROSSI

Thank you. It was a great pleasure.

MR. MC ILHENNY
(*As they go into the Pensione*)
Arrivederci.

MRS. MC ILHENNY

Arrivederci . . . ! Why, Lloyd McIlhenny!

MR. MC ILHENNY
(*Pushing her in*)
Oh, for Pete's sake, Edith, don't make such a fuss!
(*And the door closes after them.*)

LEONA

I know a little shop where Mrs. McIlhenny could have saved 3,000 lira.

DI ROSSI

I did not run out and have that glass made for you.

LEONA

Of course not. It's eighteenth century, cookie!

DI ROSSI

Do not call me "cookie"!

LEONA

It's politer than some other names that come to mind.
(*She walks away.*)

DI ROSSI

Now you are angry!

LEONA

Nope.

DI ROSSI

And suspicious again.

LEONA

Angry, no. Suspicious, yes!

DI ROSSI

I tell you now: You can always find something to be suspicious of in anyone!

LEONA

All right, I can! And this doesn't help!

DI ROSSI

Suspicion will never . . .

LEONA

What do you want me to feel? How do you expect me to feel?

DI ROSSI

(*Going back to table, takes out goblet*)
In Venetian glass, the same design is used over and over for years and years. That is true! That goblet *is* eighteenth century. It is not true that I had to search for it. (*Puts goblet back and goes to her*) I had it yesterday when you came. I wanted to be sure I could see you again. You can believe me or not. . . . No. Believe me, please.

LEONA

. . . I used to believe advertisements. Then I got in the business.

DI ROSSI

But I am not selling anything. I am not anything to sell!
I would like to be with you so we could know us better. What
happens after that, happens—or does not happen.

LEONA

If you were trying to convince someone else, I could even
help you.

DI ROSSI

But you cannot help me with you. (*She is silent and turns
away. A pause, then:*) Peccato. And you didn't even admire
the shirt.

LEONA
(*Turns*)

What shirt?

DI ROSSI
(*Touching his*)

It is silk. I borrowed it from my brother so I would be fine
and elegant for you. Pure silk.

LEONA

Really?

DI ROSSI
(*A step toward her*)

Sure. Feel!

LEONA
(*A step toward him, feels shirt*)

It is. Beautiful.

DI ROSSI

And you did not even know.

LEONA

I'm sorry.

(*She touches his arm on this. He covers her hand with his.*)

DI ROSSI

Prego. Have some coffee with me this evening. It is a beginning to hear music with someone. (*She moves to withdraw her hand*) Relax. Relax and the world is beautiful. (*Releases her hand*) Take a deep breath, like for singing. (*He inhales. She smiles*) It is not very much to have coffee with me, is it?

LEONA

No.

DI ROSSI

Then I may come for you?

LEONA
(*Chuckles*)

I'd be honored.

DI ROSSI
(*Smiles*)

Grazie. (*Kisses her hand lightly*) Arrivederci.

LEONA

Arrivederci. (*Stopping him just before he leaves*) Signor Di Rossi . . . (*She hesitates, then says something else*) What time will you be here?

DI ROSSI

A bit before nine.

LEONA

All right.

DI ROSSI

Is there something else?

LEONA

. . . No.

DI ROSSI

Until later, then.

(*She watches him go out and over the bridge, then stares at her package. She takes out the goblet as* FIORIA *comes out of the Pensione.*)

FIORIA

(*The inevitable cigarette dangling from her lips.
Going to canal door*)

I wanted to come out before, but I heard a man's voice. Ah, you found another goblet!

LEONA

Yes.

FIORIA

Very handsome. Very, very handsome.

LEONA

Do you know anything about Venetian glass?

FIORIA

I have lived here all my life.

LEONA

Is this eighteenth century?

FIORIA

(*Takes it*)

Yes it is. (*Shrugs as she hands it back*) But it is so lovely, what is the difference?

(*Turns to close the canal doors.*)

Curtain

ACT ONE

Scene III

It is evening. The garden is soft and dusky; only a few of the little lights glow in the shadows. Delicate bells chime and, from somewhere along the canal, sweet music is heard.

A young man is in the garden, a boy, really, in a white sports shirt, slacks and sandals. He is leaning pleasantly against the tree, finishing a cigarette. There is a cry, soft and romantic now of "Gondola, Gondola!" from the canal. THE BOY *hears only the music; he hums a few bars, then stops as a light goes on in the open hallway of the Pensione. He snuffs out his cigarette against the tree and puts the stub in his pocket.* LEONA *appears in the doorway wearing something pretty, but not fancy; her appointment is not yet an occasion.*

She peers around puzzled, then takes a few steps into the garden.

THE BOY
(In a soft voice and quite good English)
Miss Samish . . .

LEONA

Oh, hello!

THE BOY

Good evening.

71

LEONA

Don't tell me you found some more goblets.

THE BOY

(*Smiling, too*)

No. I bring a message.

LEONA

Signor Di Rossi can't make it.

THE BOY

Oh, no. He will be here, but he must be a little late.

LEONA

It's very nice of you to come and tell me.

THE BOY

We have no telephone and this is on the way to the piazza.

LEONA

Sit down.

THE BOY

(*Shyly*)

No . . .

LEONA

(*Sitting at table*)

Come on. The concert doesn't begin until nine. Or aren't you going to hear the music?

THE BOY

(*Sitting*)

Well, I will hear it—(*Laughs*)—while I am walking around. Music is very helpful, with the girls. (*Points to canal*) Like that.

LEONA

Where is that coming from?

THE BOY

They play in the gondolas.

LEONA

That's nice. Would you like some coffee?

THE BOY

No, thank you.

LEONA

Cigarette?

THE BOY

American?

LEONA

Be my guest.

THE BOY

Thank you. I will save it for later, if you don't mind. American cigarettes are marvelous. Permit me. (*Lights a match for hers; getting expansive*) This is quite luxurious here, but nothing compared to America.

LEONA

Have you been to America?

THE BOY

No, but everything in America is better. I am intending to go there soon. Soon as I can get enough money. But all the money is in America. It's a problem.

LEONA

Don't you like working for Signor Di Rossi?

THE BOY

Very much. Many Americans come in. Americans are marvelous. Everybody has money.

LEONA

Not quite everybody, cookie. Tell me: do you think the Signor is a nice man?

THE BOY

Oh, yes. He likes you very much, too. (*She laughs*) And he is very particular. He thinks you are marvelous.

LEONA

Not marvelous.

THE BOY

Is that not a good word? An American lady used it. But I was too young.

LEONA

How old are you now?

THE BOY

Older.
     (*They laugh.*)

LEONA

The Signor didn't really say I was marvelous, now did he?

THE BOY

Perhaps not, but it is clear he thinks so.

LEONA

Why?

THE BOY

You had only to see how upset he was that he would be late for you. He did not want to be, but my most little sister—she got ill and he had to take her to the doctor. It is nothing serious, nothing at all, but he always worries about the children. He is a very excellent father, you know.

LEONA

No, I didn't know.

THE BOY

Oh, marvelous!

LEONA

He worries about whose children?

THE BOY

His. Us.

LEONA

You?

THE BOY

I am Vito.

LEONA

(Puts out cigarette, rises)

Vito Di Rossi. His son.

THE BOY

(Rises)

Yes!

LEONA

And your mother?

VITO

She is fine.

LEONA

So am I. Except for the hole in my head.
(She moves to steps.)

VITO

(Follows. Worried)

Miss Samish, Papa married very young. His hair was like
that when he . . .

LEONA

(*Turns to him*)

Cookie—you better tell Papa not to come.

VITO

But Papa won't be very long.

LEONA

Tell him not to come!

VITO

. . . Yes, Miss Samish. (*Starts out rear door, turns back*)
Perhaps I can tell him to come tomorrow night?

LEONA

I don't think so.

VITO

He will be very disappointed.

LEONA

Mama will be glad.

VITO

My mama? Why?

LEONA

. . . I just don't understand anything, not a thing!

VITO

Papa could explain.

LEONA

(*Turns on him*)

You tell him not to come.

VITO

Yes, Miss Samish.

LEONA

You hear me?

VITO

Yes, Miss Samish.
> (*He goes. During the following, he ascends the stone footbridge from the calle and crosses it and disappears.* LEONA *stands aimlessly. The music has stopped some time ago. Bells ring occasionally.* GIOVANNA *comes cheerfully out of the Pensione carrying a tray with two cups of demi-tasse and sugar.*)

GIOVANNA

Signorina, non vuole del caffè? (LEONA *stares*) Caffè.
> (*She pantomimes, with gusto, drinking coffee.*)

LEONA

Si. Prego.

GIOVANNA

Qui?
> (*Points vigorously to table.*)

LEONA

Si. Prego.

GIOVANNA
> (*Puts tray on table*)

Va bene. (*Turns to go in; then, gently:*) Signorina, che cosa è?

LEONA
> (*Smiling a little*)

Nothing. Niente, Giovanna. Grazie. (*Taking a step closer*) Giovanna . . . Signor e Signora Yaeger . . .

GIOVANNA

Si . . .

LEONA

Ah . . . Where? . . . Dove?

GIOVANNA

In loro stanza.
(*Points upstairs in the Pensione.*)

LEONA

Grazie.
(*Starts to the Pensione but* GIOVANNA *stops her.*)

GIOVANNA

No! Signor Yaeger—(*Angry tones:*)—rararararararararara.
Signora Yaeger—(*Imitating crying*)—wahwahwahwah. (*Clapping her hands to her face:*) Terrible! (GIOVANNA *turns, pointing, only to see* JUNE *who has come into the doorway*) Mi scusi. Lei vuole del caffè, Signora?

JUNE

Per favore.

GIOVANNA

Subito.
(*Grimaces to* LEONA *and hurries inside.*)

JUNE
(*Apologetically*)
Marital troubles.

LEONA

I wish I had 'em. Matter of fact, I do.

JUNE

If you're going to be nice, I'm going to cry again.

LEONA

You cry, I'm sunk.

JUNE

Not you!

LEONA

Of course not me. I'm a million laughs. All from the heart.

JUNE

(*Looks at her, unable to tell if* LEONA *is serious. Then:*)
Everyone just loves you.

LEONA

I know.

JUNE

They do.

LEONA

I don't want everyone. (*Then, smiling*) I can't handle a
crowd.

JUNE

I can even handle—(*Starting to cry*)—oh, here I go again.

LEONA

(*Seating her at table*)
Well, go in comfort. (*Getting* JUNE *a handkerchief*) Don't
be ashamed in front of me, cookie. I'm almost glad it
happened, whatever it was. With you and Eddie, it couldn't
be anything serious, and it gives us a chance to get closer. The
three of us could be great buddies, you know.

JUNE

It wasn't anything serious. Giovanna's a terrible exaggerator.
Eddie and I weren't fighting like she said.

LEONA

(*Sitting*)
They're all exaggerators.

JUNE

He's having trouble working, so he's a little testy, that's all. No sugar for me.

LEONA

I'll only take one lump. I ran out of saccharin.

JUNE

Everything goes crazy for me.

LEONA

"Everything": one quarrel.

JUNE

Not only one. Everything always does go crazy. It did with my other husband, too.

LEONA

Your other husband?

JUNE

Oh, yes. I'm a loser once already. A musician.

LEONA

At least, you're faithful to the arts.

JUNE

Not that kind of a musician. Skipper played saxophone. That pays very well, you know.

LEONA

I never in a million years would've guessed you were married before.

JUNE

It was just as lovely in the beginning with Skipper. I must do something because all of a sudden with him, too—everything went crazy. If he wasn't playing cards all night, he was drinking. So I cleared out.

LEONA

Why?

JUNE

A man does things like that, he doesn't love you enough.
I have to be everything to someone I love.

LEONA

(*Gets up*)
You have to be everything.

JUNE

Is that crazy?

LEONA

Yes. And you're crazy to complain. Good, bad, indifferent,
there are two of you, cookie.

JUNE

What do you mean?

LEONA

Two. That's the nicest number in the world. You're two
now and you were before. Don't push your luck too far.
Everything doesn't go crazy—you just ask too much.
(*She walks away.*)

JUNE

What's the matter? What did I say wrong?

LEONA

Nothing. It's me.

JUNE

Something happened to you.

LEONA

Not a thing. That's my history. (*Goes back to table, gets her
purse*) Come on, I'll treat you to a pick-up. We're in Venice,

cookie. Sometimes, I'm just walking down an alley and it hits me: I finally made it! I'm in Europe. I'm in Venice, Italy! What do you say we jump into our Bikinis and go swimming in Harry's Bar? You, me and El Groucho. That'll fix up all of us.

JUNE

Not Eddie.

LEONA

(*Going to house*)

I'll rout him out.

JUNE

(*Gets up and stops her*)

No. He'd rather be alone.

LEONA

Oh. O.K. How about you and me?

JUNE

When I feel like this, I kind of always go to the movies.

LEONA

Even in Venice?

JUNE

Movies are movies.

LEONA

. . . What's playing?

JUNE

I don't know.

LEONA

Doesn't it matter?

JUNE

It's probably an American picture. They're much better in Italian . . . Would you like to come?

LEONA

At home, I go once in six months. Well, I came to Europe for a change, didn't I? I'll walk with you and see what's playing.

(*As they start to leave by the rear door,* FIORIA *comes out of the Pensione smoking a cigarette and carrying a cup of coffee.*)

FIORIA

Buona sera.

LEONA

Buona sera.

FIORIA

I thought you were going out this evening, Miss Samish.

LEONA

I am. I'm going to the movies with my girl friend.

(*She takes* JUNE's *arm and they stroll off.* FIORIA *sits at table. Again, chimes in the distance. She is putting out her cigarette when* EDDIE *appears in the doorway, his hands in his pockets. After a bit, he wanders into the garden.*)

FIORIA

She has gone to the cinema with Miss Samish.

(*He gives no reaction, just looks up at the sky. Then he comes to the table and stares at her.*)

EDDIE

You're always on hand after we have a fight.

FIORIA

Yes. I am always on hand.

EDDIE

What about Signor Faustino?

FIORIA

What about il Signor Faustino?

EDDIE

How'd you get rid of him?

FIORIA

I do not have to get rid of him.

EDDIE

I thought you saw him every night when he's in town.

FIORIA

Signor Faustino is an intellectual, so he loves to talk too
much. My husband also was an intellectual and loved to talk
too much. They two used to talk too much together. It was
very amusing.

EDDIE

Was it.

FIORIA

They never talked about me.

EDDIE

You and Faustino were friends even while your husband
was alive.

FIORIA

You are so delicate.

EDDIE

And your husband knew.

FIORIA

I am not certain. I would think Yes.

EDDIE

It didn't bother him. Or Faustino. Or least of all you.

FIORIA

You have such impractical morality. In Italy, there is not divorce, there is only discretion.

EDDIE

You think after a fight, I'll be available.

FIORIA

I think after a fight, you may be available. You were once before.

EDDIE

So I may be again.

FIORIA

I hope that.

EDDIE

Why?

FIORIA

It was very pleasant that other time.

EDDIE
(*Softer*)

Was it?

FIORIA

Didn't you find it so?

EDDIE

You know I did.

FIORIA

I answer the same.

EDDIE

Listen—I don't love you.

FIORIA

Who asked?

EDDIE

You wouldn't, but I have to say it.

FIORIA
(*Smiling*)

Yes: you have to be honest. You have to let me know you
will not give me anything. I know. (*Laughs*) My God, you
people—you worry about the most idiotic things!
(*Rises.*)

EDDIE
(*Grinning*)

Do we indeed?

FIORIA

You in particular.
(*He looks at her a moment, then goes to canal door.*)

EDDIE
(*Calls*)

Mauro! Mauro! (*Comes back to her*) Don't you ask anything?

FIORIA

Of course. I ask you to risk trouble with your wife. I ask
you not to feel guilty. I ask you to enjoy yourself—so I will
enjoy myself.

EDDIE

I will. I am.

FIORIA

So am I . . .

MAURO
(*Comes in from the gondola landing*)
Buona sera. You want gondola again?

EDDIE

Si.

MAURO
(*Opens door*)

Okey-dokey.

EDDIE

Signora . . .

FIORIA

Signor . . .
(*Together, they walk through the canal door which
MAURO holds for them. As FIORIA and EDDIE are going
through, the rear door opens and LEONA enters the
garden. Their backs are to her. She stops dead, watching them disappear down the steps and then watching the canal door close after them. Laughter comes
from beyond the wall. Then, after a time, the door
opens and MAURO comes out. He carefully closes the
door and stands in the garden counting the lira notes
he holds in his hand. On the little footbridge, DI ROSSI
appears. He looks briefly down into the canal, then
into the garden, then hurries across the bridge and
descends into the calle. MAURO looks up from his
money and sees LEONA who has not moved. He grins.*)

MAURO

Hey, lady, wanna buy American cigarettes? Chestyfield!

LEONA

(*Grabs the boy's wrist in fury*)

What did you get that money for?

MAURO

Is mine!

LEONA

What did you get it for?

MAURO

Leggo!
  (*Yanks away.*)

LEONA

That's dirty!

MAURO

Is money!

LEONA

(*Advancing on him*)

You mustn't do that any more!

MAURO

I work, I get pay!

LEONA

(*Grabbing him*)

Is that what you do? (*Shaking him*) Is that your work?

MAURO

Whassa matter wit' you, whassa matter?

LEONA

You stop that, you stop that *now*!
(DI ROSSI *has entered. Quickly, he goes to them and pulls*
LEONA *away*.)

DI ROSSI

What happened? What did he do?

MAURO
(*Almost in tears*)

Nothing!

DI ROSSI

Sta zitto!

LEONA

He's a child, a baby. And just one minute ago . . .
(*She points to the canal door.*)

DI ROSSI

Oh, Signora Fioria and the young painter. (LEONA *stares*
at him. He smiles) I saw from the bridge. For that, you are
angry at a child?
(*She turns away.*)

MAURO

Whassa matter?

DI ROSSI

You work for the gondolier?

MAURO

Si. Che cosa ho fatto?

DI ROSSI

Niente. Va a cada.
(*The kid picks up some of his money which he dropped in the tussle. He is defiant, and trying not to bawl.*)

MAURO

I work, I get pay.

DI ROSSI

Va bene, va bene.

MAURO

All time before, she nice. Friend. Now—now— (*Confronting* LEONA) Whassa matter, lady, you crazy?

LEONA

Si.

MAURO

Is not funny!

LEONA

Mauro . . .
(*She steps toward him, holding out her hands.*)

MAURO

No!

LEONA

(*As she gets pack of cigarettes from table*)
I'm sorry, Mauro. You work, you get pay. I'm very sorry, cookie . . . O.K.?

MAURO
(*Coldly*)

O.K.

LEONA

You want Chestyfield?

MAURO
(*Hesitates, then grins at her*)

Two?

LEONA

Two.

MAURO

Grazie.

LEONA

Prego.

MAURO

You okey-dokey now, lady?

LEONA

Yes.

MAURO

Be seein' ya.

LEONA

Be seein' ya. (MAURO *goes out the rear door; she does not look at* DI ROSSI) Something happens to this city at night. (*Throws pack of cigarettes on table and moves over to canal door.*)

DI ROSSI

Are you going to be angry at Venice now? Your friend Eddie would do the same in Kansas City.

LEONA

Not in a gondola.

DI ROSSI

That is an advantage of Venice. Miss Samish, you were shocked.

LEONA

No. Disappointed.

DI ROSSI

No. Shocked.

LEONA
(*Turns on him, sharply*)
I don't like dishonesty.

DI ROSSI

You are not his wife.

LEONA

She's at the movies, fortunately. Didn't Vito give you **my** message?

DI ROSSI
(*Smiling*)

Yes.

LEONA

He isn't your nephew any more than he's your niece!

DI ROSSI

Ah, I see, I see.

LEONA

Why didn't you tell me you were married?

DI ROSSI

I was too vain.

LEONA

Too vain!

DI ROSSI

Vito makes me seem too old.

LEONA

With me, you wouldn't exactly be robbing the cradle!
That's not the reason you didn't tell me!

DI ROSSI

What is?

LEONA

. . . You knew how I'd feel.

DI ROSSI
(*Gently*)

No. But I was afraid. I was afraid if you knew too soon,
you would end us before we began. . . . Now I am afraid
I was right.
(*A pause.*)

LEONA
(*Indicating the canal*)

No wonder you approve of that—Albany night boat.

DI ROSSI

I am in approval of living. Miss Samish, I have been married many years—many. But for eight, nine, ten, I don't know,
we have not loved.

LEONA

Ha. How old is your youngest child?

DI ROSSI

Is that a question of love? We also speak together and eat
together. Even if a divorce were possible, we could not get
one. We have too many children and too little money. So—
I live outside.

LEONA

That's not right.

DI ROSSI
(*Bewildered*)

Why?

LEONA

It just isn't.

DI ROSSI

Because it is not what you Americans do! Because it is different! Va bene! It is what we do but not what you do. It is neither right *nor* wrong. Right and wrong do not exist in the air, Miss Samish! Americans may live—

LEONA

We live, don't you worry.

DI ROSSI

Ah, then it is not wrong!

LEONA

It's your attitude! Pretending anything is fine and dandy just because you want to do it.

DI ROSSI

Thank you. Now I see. It is fine to *do* as long as you feel bad about doing it. You Americans go so on and on about the sex.

LEONA

We don't take it lightly.

DI ROSSI

Take it, don't talk it!

LEONA

Is that what your wife does?

DI ROSSI

You are obsessed with my wife!

LEONA

Does she have friends?

DI ROSSI

Naturally!

LEONA

Like Signora Fioria does?

DI ROSSI

No!

LEONA

Oh? Why not?

DI ROSSI

My wife is a mother!

LEONA

Ah, I see, I see, I see. Signor, you were shocked.

DI ROSSI

No. Disappointed.

LEONA

No. Shocked.

DI ROSSI

I am glad your sense of humor is returning.

LEONA

I'm sorry yours is going.

DI ROSSI

(*Angrily*)

You talk like a silly school child! My wife has not a thing
to do with us! Nor Signora Fioria, nor your friends, nor anyone. Lucky for us no one else matters. Only you and I.
Only we are important!

LEONA

You've managed to make me feel very unimportant.

DI ROSSI

(*Goes to her*)

How? How?

LEONA

What am I supposed to be to you?

DI ROSSI

Must I be a husband?

LEONA

No!

DI ROSSI

Then whatever you wish!

LEONA

Whatever I wish . . .

DI ROSSI

You will never never find romance by being romantic.
Never! Yes, I am using the right words. In English! I know
very well what you wish. You come here, you ride in a gondola, and you sigh, Ah, Venice! So beautiful, so romantic!
Ah, these Italians! So lyrical, so romantic, such children! And
you dream: he is young, handsome, rich, witty, brilliant. A
gondola of his own. A duke, or a count at the very least.

And—unmarried. Well, I am a shopkeeper. Not handsome. Not rich, not young, not witty, not brilliant. No title; no gondola. And not unmarried. But, Miss Samish, I am a man, and I want you. But you? "It's wrong, it's wicked, it's this, it's that." You are a hungry child to whom someone brings— ravioli. "But I don't want ravioli, I want beefsteak!" You are hungry, Miss Samish! Eat the ravioli!

LEONA

I'm not that hungry!

DI ROSSI

We are *all* that hungry! For what do we live? You, for- give me, you people have an expression: to save for a rainy day. Perhaps you can do that with money, but why with the emotion?

LEONA

It once rained forty days and forty nights.

DI ROSSI

And there was once a seven-year drought. Believe me, when there comes a moment out of time, something simpatico between two people—big, small, middle-sized but *something*— you must take a chance on it. You must hold on to it and try to make many, many more moments from the first. (*A pause*) The noise in your head is so loud, Miss Samish. Be quiet. Let it happen. I want it to happen.

LEONA

Don't you think I do?

DI ROSSI

Then?

LEONA

It just isn't the way I thought it would be.

DI ROSSI

I am sorry.

LEONA

No, it's me. I didn't realize I came from such a different world.

DI ROSSI

Therefore I am the wrong for you.

LEONA

(*Turns to him*)

You've talked me out of that. (*He takes a step toward her*) Almost. I wouldn't care anyway, if—I knew you really wanted me. Do you? (*He goes to her*) Don't—don't sell me. Just tell me—honestly.

DI ROSSI

I want you.

LEONA

(*Wryly*)

You know something about me? I ask, you answer, but I'm hard of hearing.

DI ROSSI

Eventually, you will hear.

LEONA

That's a long, long time.

DI ROSSI

(*Tapping her head*)

The noise again. You are wondering: *if* it happens, *will* it last? For how long?

LEONA

No. I'm not going to be here long.

DI ROSSI

So it is better to take home only Venetian glass.

LEONA

No. I want someone!

DI ROSSI

And I, too. (*He pulls her into his arms and kisses her hard. Then, he gently releases her*) For a lady from a different world, you do that very well.

LEONA

Grazie.
(*Gets her compact.*)

DI ROSSI
(*Laughs*)

You are embarrassed.

LEONA

Well, sure!
(*Fixes her lipstick.*)

DI ROSSI

Come. The concert in the piazza has started long ago.

LEONA

I've had my coffee.

DI ROSSI

Have some more.

LEONA

. . . I would like to go to Harry's Bar.

DI ROSSI

So would I.

LEONA

Then let's go.

DI ROSSI

I can't.

LEONA

I have money.

DI ROSSI

No.

LEONA

Now you're being romantic.

DI ROSSI

No. I see no reason why we should not go if one of us can pay. But you do. (*Taps his head*) You would soon begin again thinking: he is only interested in my money.

LEONA

(*Goes to him*)

No. I've given up thinking for Lent. (*Taking money from her bag*) I'd rather give you this here. Is it enough?

DI ROSSI

Are you planning to get drunk?

LEONA

No.

DI ROSSI

It is enough. (*She fixes her make-up. He holds up the money*) You are trying hard to be what you think is Venetian. Aren't you?

LEONA

Yes, I'm trying. Mama used to say: Enjoy yourself, it's too late already. (*Puts the compact in her bag*) I have cigarettes. (*In a sudden angry assertion of pride,* DI ROSSI *grabs her to him again and kisses her. From the distant piazza come faint chords of music. He releases her abruptly.*)

DI ROSSI

I have my own cigarettes.

LEONA
(*Trying to joke*)

Chestyfield? (*He says nothing. She takes a handkerchief from her bag, wipes her lips, then his, saying:*) Don't let me spoil this.

DI ROSSI
(*Smiles, takes her hand*)

I can be a child, too. Ready?

LEONA

Yes.
(*She closes her bag, then suddenly looks at him.*)

DI ROSSI

What is it?

LEONA

I was just wondering . . .

DI ROSSI

What?

LEONA
(*With a smile*)
Whether I was ravioli.

DI ROSSI
(*Smiling, too*)
No. But, Miss Samish, I *like* ravioli!
(*She takes his arm and they start off as the music comes up and*

The Curtain Falls

ACT TWO

ACT TWO

Scene I

Late afternoon but the garden still glows with sunlight. A table and two chairs left of center. There is a chaise-longue-like canvas chair at right. FIORIA *and* LEONA *are having a drink.* FIORIA *is dressed casually, but* LEONA *has changed for dinner. The voluminous saddle bag has been replaced by a small evening bag into which she is trying to cram a thick wad of lira notes. Now she folds them for another try.*

FIORIA

How much did you get altogether?

LEONA

For the hundred bucks? Sixty-five thousand lira.

FIORIA

That's a very good rate.

LEONA

Well, Di Rossi's black-market man is very good—and very legitimate. (*Rises, looking at the roll*) You know, this *could* choke a small horse. Cockeyed like everything else. Di Rossi wouldn't take a perfectly legitimate commission for the money he exchanged for me, but it's all right to go to a restaurant and . . . (*Cuts herself off and closes the bag*) Fabulous city you have here, Signora.

105

FIORIA

You like it now.

LEONA
(*Looks at her watch*)

Si.

FIORIA

What did you sight-see today?

LEONA

Niente. I didn't have time.
(*Holds the watch to her ear.*)

FIORIA

Bene!

LEONA

Did the phone ring when I was taking my bath?

FIORIA

I think so, yes.

LEONA

It wasn't for me.

FIORIA

Giovanna answered so we will probably never know. When
he is coming for you?

LEONA
(*Looks at watch*)

Ten minutes ago.

FIORIA

One can't always close a shop as early as one would like.

LEONA

It doesn't really matter. Signora, do you know the Mrs. Di Rossi?

FIORIA

No. I have heard she was once rather pretty but now is very fat. (*Gently*) Miss Samish, why make problems? In Italy . . .

LEONA

I know: In Italy . . . It'd be great if you could come here from America with nothing but a suitcase. But—you don't come over that way.

FIORIA

So it is hard to understand us.

LEONA

(*From the canal, comes the cry "Gondola, Gondola!"*)
Yes.
(*The eyes of the two women meet.*)

FIORIA

(*After a moment, carefully*)
How was the film last night?

LEONA

I didn't go. I'd seen it. (*Again the cry: "Gondola, Gondola!"*) June said she had a marvelous time. She cried her eyes out.

FIORIA

(*Laughs*)
I love to cry in the cinema.

LEONA

I cry at cartoons.

FIORIA

How splendid! (*Casually*) What did you do last night?

LEONA

Signor Di Rossi came.

FIORIA

Last night and again tonight. (*Bells chime and* LEONA *again glances at her watch*) Miss Samish! The miracle magical!

LEONA
(*Sits down*)

Not quite. I used to think when I fell in love, I'd hear a waltz. No waltz, Signora.

FIORIA

You should have gone to Vienna.

LEONA

I should've hired a band.

FIORIA

What you call a waltz, I hear very often. With me, it is necessary. Perhaps sometimes, I have to play it myself but—I hear it.

LEONA

When you're finished, can you stop playing?

FIORIA
(*Laughs*)

Sometimes.

LEONA

I must say that's practical. But it's not for me.

FIORIA

Because the man is a minute or two late?

LEONA

No. Lots of reasons.

FIORIA

Because he is not all you hoped for? But Miss Samish, there is something wrong with everything! Everything is imperfect! Are you then to have nothing? Listen, you make me impatient, excuse me. . . . Stop looking at the moon. Look at *here*. See the things as they are and make from them the best you can.

LEONA

Yes, the *best*.

FIORIA

Indeed the best; only a squanderer takes anything.

LEONA

I want . . . (*She smiles wryly*) The trouble is I *want*. I wish the day could come . . .
　　(*The* YAEGERS *enter the garden through the rear door, looking glowingly young and happy.* EDDIE *carries sketching materials, his arm around* JUNE.)

FIORIA

Only Americans make health look so attractive.
　　(EDDIE *drops his arm.*)

LEONA

(*To them*)

I'm glad you're cozy again.

EDDIE

Again?

JUNE

Giovanna.

FIORIA

(*Going to the garden door, rear*)
Their storms are very brief, Miss Samish.

JUNE

(*As she and* EDDIE *move to the double-deck chair*)
And it's lovely when they're over.

LEONA

Signora, if you see Giovanna, would you ask her if I had
a phone call?

FIORIA

She is more likely by the front door with Alfredo. (*Smiles*)
He will come. Be patient. I am.
    (*Exits.*)

EDDIE

Who is the He who will come?

JUNE

Signor Di Rossi. (*Pulling away from* EDDIE) I told him, you
don't mind.

LEONA

What are you building? It's nothing. And the date wasn't
that definite. (*To* EDDIE) Can I see what you did today?

EDDIE

They're just sketches.

JUNE
(Goes to EDDIE*)*

But they're darling!

LEONA
(As bells chime, she looks at her watch)

What time do you have?

EDDIE

Twenty after.

LEONA

I thought I was slow.

EDDIE

Why?

LEONA

The bells.

JUNE

The bells in Venice don't have a thing to do with time.

LEONA

Why do they ring them?

EDDIE

What else're you going to do with bells?

JUNE

Ha ha ha.

EDDIE

Ha ha ha.

LEONA

What about a drink?

EDDIE

Uh-uh. I'm on the wagon.

LEONA

When you reform, you go wild.
(*She has started for the house.*)

JUNE

Where you going?

LEONA

Just to see if I can find Giovanna. I'll be back.
(*She goes.*)
(*During the following,* EDDIE *shifts to chaise-longue-like garden chair, stretches out and pats the place beside him.* JUNE *settles down next to him in his arms. Occasionally, he kisses her hair or her cheek, she kisses his hand or his chest.*)

EDDIE

Leona's cute. She really likes that gent but she's afraid someone'll know it.

JUNE

They do have a date. She told me this morning.

EDDIE

If he doesn't show, I'll break his Venetian glasses.

JUNE

Maybe it's better if he doesn't.

EDDIE

Why?

JUNE

He's married.

EDDIE

So?

JUNE

"So!"

EDDIE

It's better than nothing. Let her live up her vacation.

JUNE

That Mr. Di Rossi'll just give both of them a good boot.

EDDIE

Both?

JUNE

Leona and Mrs. Di Rossi.

EDDIE

Maybe he loves one of them.

JUNE

Certainly not his wife.

EDDIE

He tell you?

JUNE

How can he love her and be unfaithful?

EDDIE

Has he been?

JUNE

Of course!

EDDIE

Fast worker.

JUNE

Oh, I don't know about Leona and him—but he's trying hard enough.

EDDIE
(*Sits up*)

He might still love his wife.

JUNE
(*Sits up*)

Honey, how can a man love his wife and chase somebody else?

EDDIE

Easy.

JUNE

Some loving husband who'd hurt his wife!

EDDIE

How would he hurt her?

JUNE

She'd know.

EDDIE

Not necessarily.

JUNE

Any woman knows.

EDDIE

She can sense it.

JUNE

Yes, she can!

EDDIE

Feminine intuition.

JUNE

Yes.

EDDIE
(Lies back)

Bull.

JUNE
(Lies back too)

All right.

EDDIE

Did you know I was unfaithful last night?

JUNE

Sure.

EDDIE

You did not.

JUNE

With four brunette signorinas. You told me yourself.

EDDIE

Three. Don't exaggerate.

JUNE

Only three—and you call yourself a man! *(Sits up)* What did we start fighting about last night?

EDDIE

I don't know.
(Sits up.)

JUNE

I remember you said you didn't love me. But that **was**
because you were in a bad mood.

EDDIE
(*Suddenly*)

I do love you . . .

JUNE

Then tell me what you really did last night. What's **so**
funny?

EDDIE

You. If I say I don't love you, you say I'm in a bad mood.
If I say I do love you, you say: What did you do last night.

JUNE

Well, what *did* you do?

EDDIE

I told you.

JUNE

Tell me again.

EDDIE

Checking up on the story, eh?

JUNE

Sure.

EDDIE

I went for a long walk; sat in a café and got stiff. Alone.

JUNE

You said you picked up three brunettes.

EDDIE

I was exaggerating. Only one.

JUNE

Was she pretty?

EDDIE

No.

JUNE

Attractive?

EDDIE

You might not think so.

JUNE

Intelligent?

EDDIE

Yes. Very.

JUNE

What happened?

EDDIE

(*Looks at her*)

I was unfaithful but I love you.

JUNE

You weren't really.

EDDIE

Yes, I was.

JUNE

Really?

EDDIE

Really. (*She rolls over half on him so that she is looking him in the eye. He smiles and kisses her*) No, not really. (*She smiles and lays her head on his chest. Inside the house, the telephone is ringing. The second ring is cut off by some-one answering*) What would you do if I were unfaithful?

JUNE

Kill you. No. Kill her and maybe you . . . Die, I guess.

EDDIE

It wouldn't mean I didn't love you.

JUNE

It'd mean you didn't love me enough.

EDDIE

Then I guess I don't love you enough.

JUNE

Honey, don't kid any more.

EDDIE

I'm not kidding.

JUNE

Will you stop?
(*A pause, then she digs him in the ribs.*)

EDDIE

Ow!

JUNE

That's just a sample.
(*Happily lying back.*)

LEONA

(*Coming out of the house*)
It's obvious the guy who installed the French telephone
system has been doing a little underwater work here. I just
picked it up and before I could say pronto . . . (*Inside, the
phone rings again*) Scusi!
(*She runs back in the house.*)

EDDIE

And you say it's better if Di Rossi doesn't show. Something
is better than nothing, honey.

JUNE

(*Sitting up*)
I remember what started us off last night. I didn't know
some word.

EDDIE

That isn't what it was about.

JUNE

I wish I weren't dumb.

EDDIE

You're hipped on that.

JUNE

No, I hear how you talk with other people. I must say the
more gab I hear, the less I think anybody understands any-

body else. I'll bet if people couldn't talk, they wouldn't feel so alone.

(*The lights begin to fade down.*)

EDDIE

Do you feel alone?

JUNE

Not when we talk about me. I wonder if you'd've married me if you'd known.

EDDIE

Known what?

JUNE

That I was dumb.

EDDIE

You're not dumb.

JUNE

Oh, I was smart enough to keep my mouth shut at first. A pretty girl sits and listens, a man thinks she's deep. Are you ever sorry, though?

EDDIE

Are you?

JUNE

How could *I* be?

EDDIE

Look at what you thought you were marrying.

JUNE

Don't say that! (*Throwing herself on him heavily*) I love you.

EDDIE

(*Chuckling*)

Gently, gently.

JUNE

I do. I love your chest, your stomach . . .

EDDIE

Madame!

JUNE

And your legs, every bit of you! (*Giggling as she clutches him melodramatically:*) And it's all mine, do you hear? Mine, mine, mine!

(*They are both laughing as* LEONA *comes out again. She watches them enviously, then walks to table smiling.*)

LEONA

Back to your corners. It's for you, Eddie. La Contessa di Something-eria.

EDDIE

(*Getting up*)

Oh, God! Did you say . . . ?

LEONA

I did.

EDDIE

(*Appealing to* JUNE *as he picks up his sketch pad*)

Hon . . .

JUNE
(*Getting up*)

She's *your* friend.

EDDIE

That's no lady.
(*Goes inside.*)

JUNE

Did you find Giovanna?

LEONA

No.

JUNE

Just like her. I bet he did call, too!

LEONA

I don't even know if he has a phone in the shop. It doesn't matter. (*Pouring herself a drink*) You on the wagon, too?

JUNE

No, but I don't want one.

LEONA

I must say you don't need one.

JUNE
(*Happily*)

No, I don't, do I? Oh, Leona, what a day! I didn't go to the movies last night.

LEONA

What?

JUNE

There was no last night, it never happened! (*Laughs*)
Today was better than anything. Except tonight. No. Tomorrow morning. We love mornings best.

LEONA
(*Curtly*)
Let's not go through your whole week.
(*A pause. She drinks.*)

JUNE
. . . Italians are always late, Leona.

LEONA
I said it didn't matter.

JUNE
(*Smiling*)
I wish it did.

LEONA
(*Rises*)
Well, it doesn't. And like it or not, last night *did* happen.

JUNE
You say that in a funny way.

LEONA
Cookie, don't be so sorry for me!

JUNE
I wasn't being sorry for you, Leona.
(*A moment.*)

EDDIE
(*Coming out gaily*)
The Contessa regrets you're not feeling well.

JUNE
Me?

EDDIE
That's why we can't have dinner with her.

JUNE
Thanks a lot.

EDDIE
Mind if we eat early?

JUNE
How early?

EDDIE
Like now. Then there won't be any chance of running into her.

JUNE
(*Rises, goes to rear door*)
O.K.

EDDIE
What's the matter?

LEONA
I was a little mean.

EDDIE

Why?

LEONA

Getting jealous in my old age.

EDDIE

There isn't that much to be jealous of.

JUNE

Honey, let Leona make the jokes.

EDDIE

(*To* LEONA)

Want to have dinner with us?

LEONA

No. I'll wait a little longer for Romeo.

EDDIE

Good. (EDDIE *goes to* JUNE, *saying to* LEONA) If we see Giovanna, we'll give her one in the fanny and send her home.

(*As they start out.*)

LEONA

Grazie. Ciao.

JUNE

Ciao.

(*Goes out with* EDDIE. *They go over the bridge and off. The sun is setting; the light in the garden has been growing dim. A bell chimes.* LEONA *starts back to the table when from the house comes the sound of* GIOVANNA *singing.*)

LEONA

(*Calling*)

Giovanna! Giovanna! (*The singing continues.* LEONA *starts to the house but the telephone rings*) Oh no, cookie. (*She moves swiftly but as she crosses the threshold, the ringing stops;* GIOVANNA *has answered.* LEONA *stands in the entry, hopeful, muttering at first to herself, then aloud:*) Let it be him, please let it be . . . (GIOVANNA's *giggle stops her. Wearily, she comes down the steps, into the garden, stands limply, then looks at the little footbridge, walks to where she can see through the rear door, paces back and forth, and, at last,* GIOVANNA *begins singing again. Angrily,* LEONA *calls out:*) Giovanna! (*A stride toward the Pensione*) Giovanna!

(*The lights go on in the garden and a moment later,* GIOVANNA *herself appears with a big grin.*)

GIOVANNA

Buona sera, buona sera!

LEONA

Buona sera, my aunt! I've had search parties out for you. Where've you been? Was there a call for me? (GIOVANNA *grins idiotically and now* LEONA *remembers the ghastly fact that* GIOVANNA *cannot speak English*) Oh, my sweet Lord! Giovanna . . .

GIOVANNA

Si, Signorina?

LEONA

(*With gestures, in pidgin English-Italian*)

That telefona—for me?

GIOVANNA

Ah no, Signorina. (*Gesturing back in pidgin Italian*) Telefonata non per Lei. Per me. (*Giggles*) Alfredo.

LEONA

Si. That was Alfredo. But the telefonata before. *Before.* (GIOVANNA *stares*) Momento. (*Reaches for her bag on table and gets out her language book, muttering:*) Before, before. I had to study French. Ah—prima!

GIOVANNA

Prima?

LEONA
(*Checking the word*)

Si. Prima.

GIOVANNA

Prima che?

LEONA

Prima the other telefonata.

GIOVANNA
(*Shaking her head sadly*)

Signorina Samish . . .

LEONA

Oh, Giovanna, it's important, it's terribly important. (*Puts book on table*) Ecco. Signor Di Rossi?

GIOVANNA

Si. Molto bello.

LEONA

Si. Molto bello. (GIOVANNA *looks at* LEONA, *waiting patiently for what is to come next.* LEONA *looks at her in despair, then turns away*) He probably didn't call anyway.

GIOVANNA
(*Trying to be helpful*)
Signorina, parla.

LEONA
(*Comes back to her*)
I don't know how to parla, Giovanna.

GIOVANNA

Signor Di Rossi, telefonata.

LEONA

But did he call before, while I was taking my bath? Giovanna. Guarda. (*Seats her in chair. Points to herself:*) Io—Giovanna. (GIOVANNA *nods and* LEONA *now does a charade. She imitates* GIOVANNA *singing—which makes the girl laugh—and cleaning the house. Then she imitates the sound of a telephone ring and, leaving her cleaning, moves to answer it*) Pronto . . . Signorina Samish. Momento. (*To* GIOVANNA) Capisce?

GIOVANNA

Si, si. Molto bene!

LEONA
(*Continuing the charade, she runs up an imaginary flight of stairs and knocks on a door*)
Signora Samish? . . . Signorina Samish? (*Turns to* GIOVANNA *and points to herself*) Adesso, io Signorina Samish.

(*Now she imitates herself humming as she washes in the tub. Points to herself*) Adesso, io Giovanna. (*Again, knocks on door. No answer because—change of character, she is bathing—back to door, calls:*) Signorina Samish? (*No answer, shrugs, down the stairs and back to the telephone*) No, no Signorina Samish . . . Chi? Ah, Signor Di Rossi! . . . Si. Si, Signor. Si . . . Buon giorno.

(LEONA *hangs up and turns hopefully to* GIOVANNA *who is watching like a child. The performance over,* GIOVANNA *grins and breaks into loud applause.*)

GIOVANNA
(*Rises*)
Bravo, bravo, Signorina, bravo!

LEONA
(*Close to tears*)
Oh, Giovanna. Did he call?

GIOVANNA
(*Gently*)
No, Signorina. Telefonata per la Signora Fioria, non per Lei. Per Lei, non Signor Di Rossi.
(*From beyond the garden comes a thin, plaintive Neapolitan tune.*)

LEONA
For me no Signor Di Rossi. For me no signor . . . Well, what's so special about Venice? (*Turns to her; letting out*) But he should've called, and he should've come! It's not fair, Giovanna! Everybody's got someone, it's not fair! Why can't I? Why can't it be? It doesn't have to be perfect, just a little, just a little is all I—
(*She stops dead for* DI ROSSI *is hurrying into the garden.*)

DI ROSSI

Leona, I am sorry I am so very late. Excuse me. (*He is panting as he goes to her and kisses her hand. With affectionate happiness,* GIOVANNA *goes into the house*) It was impossible. Never, never in my life, I have bargained so hard. (*He is fishing a tissue-papered parcel from his jacket and, unwrapping it, moves to table.* LEONA *just stands, looking at him*) Three times, I walked out of his store and three times, he followed me into the street. Fortunately! Impossible man, Signor Papini. But—it was worth it, yes? (*He is holding up a necklace.* LEONA *stares at it*) It is granate, Leona. Garnets —don't you like it? (*She has been trembling and now, she bursts into tears and runs into his arms*) Oh, Leona . . . Carissima! (*He kisses her hair, caresses her back as she cries. Then:*) What did you say? I can't hear you . . . What? (*She moves her head and now, although we cannot hear what she says, he can. He smiles tenderly and holds her closer, saying softly:*) Ah, mia cara. I am happy, too!

(*The music sounds louder now, loud enough for us to hear what* LEONA *is hearing finally—a waltz.*)

Curtain

ACT TWO

Scene II

The late afternoon sun has just set and the garden lights are lit. Paper lanterns have been strung through the arbor and tree. LEONA *is giving a cocktail party. There is a large glass pitcher of martinis and the ingredients for more; toothpicked olives; a platter of antipasto. There is even music coming from an old phonograph on footstool against the wall, of, "Would You Like to Take a Walk?"*

The party has reached that euphoric stage where everyone is delighted with everyone else. GIOVANNA *has gone beyond this and is allowing* MAURO *to push her around the floor in a fairly recognizable facsimile of a dance. He is grim determination, but she giggles wildly. The* YAEGERS, FIORIA *and* DI ROSSI *watch with affectionate amusement.*

FIORIA

She won't let him lead.

EDDIE

How can you tell?

FIORIA

Tighter, Mauro!

131

DI ROSSI

He is too serious. Riposate, Mauro!

JUNE

English, Signor! Leona said only English.

DI ROSSI

Then you cannot call me Signor. You must say Renato.

FIORIA

What is Renato in English?

EDDIE

Melvin.

JUNE

No!

EDDIE

Come on, Mauro! A big finish!
(*He sings with the music which is ending. The dance finishes to much applause, laughing calls of Bravo! Bis! Encore!* MAURO *turns from* GIOVANNA *in disgust.*)

MAURO

She no good.

JUNE

You were both sensational!

EDDIE

Sure! Have a drink.

JUNE

Honey!

MAURO

No. Taste lousy.

(*He prefers to filch antipasto.* FIORIA *has gone inside for a moment.* GIOVANNA *holds out her glass to* EDDIE *for a refill.*)

DI ROSSI

Do you always have the martini at cocktail parties in America?

JUNE

Oh, yes!

DI ROSSI

Do they always taste like this?

JUNE

Oh, yes!

DI ROSSI

Fantastic. (GIOVANNA, *to* EDDIE'S *fascination, downs her martini in one gulp and hands glass back, giggles, crosses the garden and abruptly sits on the ground. During this* FIORIA *has returned*) Where is our hostess?

FIORIA

In the kitchen. She will not let me in. Ah, Giovanna! I'm afraid tomorrow we get our own breakfast.

EDDIE

Who's going to have breakfast? (*Holds up pitcher*) Hands, please.

JUNE
(Raising her empty glass)
While you're up.

FIORIA
And I, please!
(He takes her glass and JUNE'S.*)*

DI ROSSI
(Holding drink)
Eddie, you are an excellent barman. And this is the pleasantest bar I have been in. To? In.

JUNE
Renato, you're nice. Why don't you move in? *(Then, realizing)* Oh.
(Claps hand over her mouth.)

DI ROSSI
(Laughs)
You must everyone come see my house sometime. No. I must first move to a house with a garden like this and have music like yours.
*(*EDDIE *hands* JUNE *her drink.)*

FIORIA
The phonograph is Giovanna's. But an American student sent the records. He was very nice. *(*EDDIE *hands her her drink)* Thank you. He came for a fortnight and stayed three months. In winter!

JUNE
Does it ever snow in Venice?

DI ROSSI

Oh, yes!

JUNE

Often?

DI ROSSI

Oh, yes!

JUNE AND EDDIE

Fantastic!
(*They laugh.*)

FIORIA

Eddie, you know, he looked like you.

EDDIE

Who?

FIORIA

(*Getting up*)

That nice student. Yes, very much like you. His hair **was**
lighter. (*She ruffles* EDDIE's *hair*) His nose was longer.
(*She runs her finger down* EDDIE's *nose.*)

EDDIE

Tickles.

FIORIA

(*Holding his chin critically*)

His mouth was stronger. But you are better looking. (*To*
JUNE) Isn't he?

JUNE

Much.

EDDIE

How do you know?

FIORIA

We have similar taste.

JUNE

Aren't you going to let him have his chin back?

FIORIA

Oh, forgive me!
(*Sits down.*)
(*From inside comes* LEONA's *voice chanting:* "Fee Fi Fo Feeny, I smell the blood of a dry martini." *As she chants, she comes out dressed to the nines, wearing the garnet necklace and carrying a large tray of hors d'oeuvres. She is high.*)

LEONA
(*Singing as she goes to table*)

Good eating, friends!

DI ROSSI

It is about time.

JUNE

Hors d'oeuvres! Leona!

LEONA

A mere truffle.

EDDIE
(Pantomimes shooting her)

Pam pam.

LEONA

Cookie left her glass in the kitchen. *(To Eddie)* But it was bare, Father Hubbard.

EDDIE

Coming up!
(Mixes her a fresh drink.)

FIORIA
(As LEONA puts a plate on table)

Paté!

JUNE

Caviar!

EDDIE

Save some for baby!

FIORIA

Where did you find all this?

LEONA

I have a friend who gets me around. (DI ROSSI *bows*) You're charming, friend. *(Turns to EDDIE who comes and takes a sandwich)* You're charming, too. Did I show you my necklace? Garnets. Real. Bite 'em.

EDDIE
(A mouthful of food)

Delicious.

LEONA

Listen, bud, I said you were charming.

JUNE

The necklace is beautiful!

LEONA

Now you really are charming. Did I tell you who gave it to me?

EDDIE AND JUNE

Uh-huh.

LEONA
(*To* DI ROSSI)

Did I thank you for it?

DI ROSSI

Not in the last ten minutes.

LEONA

Scusami.

DI ROSSI

English, English!

FIORIA

Your own rules!

LEONA

Pardon, pardon. (*Going to* DI ROSSI) I'll thank you. (*Kisses him*) Thank you. You know, I'm easily the most charming person here.

JUNE

(*As she gets sandwich from table. To* EDDIE)
Try one of these, honey.

LEONA

Where's my Mauro? Mauro! (MAURO *has been guiltily de-
vouring antipasto. He shuts his full mouth. She puts tray
down*) Come on, cookie. Have some of these, they're better.
It's all right. You eat as much of everything as you can hold.
(*Now* MAURO *grins and chews openly.* EDDIE *hands* LEONA *her
drink*) You've very kind, sir. (*To* DI ROSSI) You're very
charming. (*To* JUNE) You're very pretty. (*To* FIORIA) You're
very—simpatico.

FIORIA

English!

LEONA

On me, it's English. (*Looking for* GIOVANNA) And you're
very . . . (*Peers down at her*) She's fractured! What happened?

DI ROSSI

She was dancing with Mauro.

LEONA

Oh, I missed the floor show. They've got to go on again.
Turn on the music, please, somebody. Giovanna, dance.
(*Takes a few steps herself to illustrate.* EDDIE *turns on the
record. Simultaneously,* GIOVANNA *has gotten up and* LEONA
has been saying:) Dance with Mauro. Come on.

MAURO

She no good.

LEONA
(*Leads* MAURO *to* GIOVANNA)
You can make her good, you can make her . . .
(*But* GIOVANNA *suddenly thrusts them aside, saying:*)

GIOVANNA
No Mauro. Alfredo!
(MAURO *falls back and sits in chair.*)

LEONA
Alfredo later.

GIOVANNA
(*Peering around*)
Alfredo? (*Revolving in a circle*) Alfredo! (*Then, running
out of the garden into the house*) ALFREDO!

LEONA
(*The music starts*)
There goes the floor show!

EDDIE
You dance with Mauro.

FIORIA
Yes!

LEONA
(*Putting her glass down*)
Mauro, want to dance with cookie? Come on.
(MAURO *flushes and runs behind the tree.*)

JUNE
He's shy.
(LEONA *starts to sing and dances toward* MAURO *who
peers out at her.*)

EDDIE

He has a crush on her!

LEONA

Too hard to get.
(*And she continues to sing as she dances over to* DI ROSSI *holding out her arms.*)

JUNE

Oh sing, Leona!

LEONA

Cookie wants to dance. Signor? I mean, monsieur?

DI ROSSI

Mademoiselle.
(*Holds his arms out.*)

LEONA

Well, if you insist. (*They dance.* LEONA *sings a bit, then:*)
Did I tell you you were charming?

DI ROSSI

Yes.

LEONA

Did I tell you *I'm* charming? (*He laughs. It is almost dark now. She hums a few bars, then says very softly:*) Renato—
thank you.
(*He holds her tighter.*)

JUNE

They just hit me.

FIORIA

Who?

JUNE

The martinis. (*Clapping her hands to her head*) Right here. (*Flopping back into chair*) I feel dreamy.

EDDIE

English, English.

JUNE

This is the delicate moment. You have to be very, very careful to keep feeling exactly like this.

LEONA
(*To* DI ROSSI)

Know what I want to do later?

EDDIE

Yes.

LEONA
(*Pointing at him*)

You're vulgar. (*At* JUNE) You're pretty. (*To* DI ROSSI) You're charming.

DI ROSSI

What do you want to do?

LEONA

Take a ride in a gondola.

JUNE
(*Claps her hands and gets up*)
Oh, yes! Can we come?

LEONA

No.
(*They dance.*)

JUNE

What a hostess! (*To* EDDIE *and* FIORIA) The hell with them.
Let's us get our own gondola. (FIORIA *breaks into laughter*)
What's so funny?

EDDIE

Don't look at me.

JUNE

The corners of your mouth are twitching.

EDDIE

She's breaking me up.

JUNE
(*Elegantly*)
I think you're both drunk and disgusting. Oh, lookie!
We've got company!
(*She points to a figure who has entered the garden and
is standing in the rear.* LEONA *looks over* DI ROSSI'S
*shoulder. She stops dancing and the figure comes for-
ward. It is* VITO. *She goes up to him.*)

LEONA

Oh. You.

VITO

Excuse me, Miss Samish . . .

DI ROSSI

What are you doing here?

LEONA

(*Recovering*)

Come on in, don't be afraid. (*Leads him in*) This is Vito,
everybody.

DI ROSSI

Vito . . .

VITO

Please, Miss Samish. I must speak to my father.
(*The word embarrasses* LEONA *but she laughs and putting an arm around* VITO, *says to* JUNE)

LEONA

Big for his age. He's really no older than Mauro. Where
is Mauro? (MAURO *comes forward. She leads him to* VITO)
Cookie, I have a playmate for you. This is Vito Di Rossi.
This is Mauro—
(*Covers her mouth and mumbles a name.*)

VITO

How do you do.

MAURO

How you do.

LEONA

See how well they get along?

DI ROSSI

Leona . . .

LEONA
(*Leading him around*)
This is Mrs. Yaeger. And Mr. Yaeger.

EDDIE
(*Pouring drinks*)

Hi.

LEONA
And Mrs. Fioria. Ooh, that sounds so wrong. Madame
Fioria. (*Leading him to the drink table*) No Italian spoken
here. Only English. Now come and meet Mr. Martini.

DI ROSSI
(*To* VITO)

Is someone ill?

VITO
(*Goes to him*)

Oh no, Papa.

DI ROSSI

What happened?

LEONA

Vito.
(*Hands him his drink.*)

VITO

Thank you, thank you. You are very generous, Miss Samish. This is a marvelous party. Americans give mar—

DI ROSSI
(*Leading* VITO *away*)

Vito! Cosa che?

VITO

Papini vuole il suo denaro.

LEONA
(*Following*)

Uh-uh. No Italian, boys.

DI ROSSI

Tell him tomorrow.

VITO

I did. He says you promised the money last night.

DI ROSSI
(*Realizing* LEONA's *attention, tries to lower his voice*)

Tell him tomorrow.

VITO

Papa, he's waiting right out there.

LEONA

Ask him in to have a drink!

DI ROSSI

Go send him away.

VITO

He won't go. He says either the money tonight or give
back the necklace. (*A pause. He sips his drink*) Martinis are
marvelous, Miss Sam—

DI ROSSI
(*Turns away*)
Sta zitto!

LEONA
(*After a pause*)
Renato, don't be embarrassed. You're too charming.
(*During the following, she darts about—to* DI ROSSI,
to her drink, to get her purse, etc.)

DI ROSSI
Leona . . .

LEONA
(*In an agony of humiliation*)
This is the first time I've felt at home in Venice. Cookie,
it happens every day in America. We invented it: the installment plan and the installment man. One birthday party—
I was eleven—the collector came just before the party and
took away the dining-room set. Suite, Mama called it. Why'd
I bring that up? (*Taking money from her bag*) Cookie,
smile. We're rich! This is all from your nice little black-
market man. How much do we need?

DI ROSSI
You don't—

LEONA
How much?

DI ROSSI

Most, I have paid.

LEONA

How much more?

DI ROSSI

Ten thousand.

LEONA

Worth it at half the price. (*Goes up and hands some notes to* VITO) Pay off the bloodsucker.
(VITO *goes.*)

DI ROSSI

(*Goes up to her*)
I will return it tomorrow. Thank you.
(*He takes her hand. She doesn't look at him. There is a long, awkward moment. Then* LEONA *turns from him.*)

LEONA

What happened to the band?

EDDIE

They went out for a smoke.
(*Goes to the phonograph and turns on the record.*)

LEONA

More important, what happened to my drink?

JUNE

It's right there.

LEONA
(*Picks up glass*)
Oh, there's too much air in this glass. (*Refilling it*) Who's ready for another? Junie?

JUNE
I know when I'm well off.

LEONA
That's what you think. (*Giggles and turns to* MAURO *who is sitting on the ground*) We know better, don't we? How's the weather down there? (*He laughs*) You don't say. (*To the others*) Interesting type. Works in an interesting business.

EDDIE
(*Sits down in chair at table*)
What?

LEONA
Gondolas. (*To* JUNE) There's more to a gondola than meets the eye. You ought to meet my eye.
(*Winks.*)

DI ROSSI
Dance.

LEONA
(*Smiling, puts her glass down*)
Cookie doesn't want to dance.

DI ROSSI

With me?

LEONA

Cookie wants to sing.

DI ROSSI •
(*Goes to her*)

Sing while we dance.

LEONA

Uh-uh. Cookie wants to be charming, all by herself.
(*She begins to sing, inventing where she does not
remember.*)

FIORIA

Have some pâté, Signor.

DI ROSSI
(*Goes over to canal door*)

Grazie.
(LEONA *dances about as she sings. After a few lines,*
VITO *returns to the garden.*)

VITO
(*Worried*)

Miss Samish . . .

LEONA

Uh-oh. Let me get my drink. Doom is coming, I can
smell it.
(VITO *steps forward to speak, but she waves him silent
while she gets her drink. Then she takes a gulp.*)

VITO

Miss Samish . . . (*Wavers, turns to his father*) Papa . . .
Papa, Signor Papini says her money is got good. (*Pause.*)

LEONA

Not good?

VITO

(*Shows money*)

He says counterfeit.

LEONA

(*Pause; she looks at* DI ROSSI)

All that lovely legitimate money you got for me?
(*She walks away from all of them.*)

DI ROSSI

It can't be! It can't be! (*Grabs the money from* VITO *and
goes to* LEONA. *Holding a note up to the light*) This is not
counterfeit. (*Holding up another*) This is not . . . (*But it is.
Quickly, he holds up another, another, all the notes, and all
but the first two are counterfeit. He looks helplessly at* LEONA,
*then puts the notes down on the table. Several times, he tries
to speak. Finally:*) I am so—what is the word—I am so something, I cannot think. In English. I cannot say in English.
Leona . . .
(*She stands silent and cold. Suddenly:*)

LEONA

Turn off that damn music!
(EDDIE *hurries and shuts off the phonograph.*)

DI ROSSI

Go, Vito.

VITO

Good night, Miss Samish. I wish . . . Good night.
(*Exits.*)

DI ROSSI

I apologize for my friend. I will see the black-market man
tomorrow . . .

LEONA
(*Turns on him*)

Why not tonight? Why don't you talk to him now? Why
don't you turn your charm on him? *Why don't you go?*

DI ROSSI
(*Shocked*)

Leona!

LEONA

Get out!

DI ROSSI

Leona, listen to me . . .

LEONA

I will not listen!

DI ROSSI

What has happened to you?

LEONA

I've swallowed all the ravioli talk I'm going to! You never
wanted me!

DI ROSSI

No, no!

LEONA

Not me, only *money!*

DI ROSSI

This is not . . .

LEONA

Why weren't you smarter? Why couldn't you have managed it so I wouldn't know? Why didn't you ask? Why didn't
you steal? Why didn't you let me alone? Why did you tell
me lies you knew I wanted to hear?

DI ROSSI

Not lies! Era vero, era vero! Tutto quello che ho detto . . .

LEONA

English, English!

DI ROSSI

I cannot in English!

LEONA

No. You couldn't in Italian!

DI ROSSI

To you, no; to you, no! You are too drunk!

LEONA

There's the old charm!

DI ROSSI

If I only want money, there is many tourist richer than
you!

LEONA

Maybe you had to take what you could get, like the rest of us!

DI ROSSI

What are you doing to us? (*She turns away*) This is ugly and stupid! I . . . (*To others*) Forgive me.
(*He goes.*)

LEONA

(*Following him to door*)
Sure! I can't fire you, you quit! (*She stands a moment, then gets her glass. A pause. Then:*) Ohh, Leona Samish, what a big rumpus *you* raised. Whatever happened to your sense of humor? Anybody see my sense of humor? (*Calling*) Oh, sense of hu—
(*But her voice breaks. She sits apart from the others. A moment, then:*)

JUNE

How could he tell so quick it was phony?

EDDIE

No watermark.

FIORIA

There is so much counterfeit money in Italy.

EDDIE

Too many unemployed artists.

FIORIA

One should examine every big note one gets. But one becomes lazy . . .

EDDIE

This one doesn't get any big notes.

FIORIA

Nor this one.

LEONA

What charming repartee! What tact! What delicacy! Shake well and add laughter.

JUNE

There's nothing to laugh at, Leona.

LEONA

There's me. I think I'm hilarious. First I coy around like a sixteen-year-old: "Look at the necklace cookie got for a present." Then I have to buy the present myself. Then it turns out my money is phony. That's highly comical. *Why don't you laugh?*

JUNE

We don't think it's funny.

EDDIE

I don't think it's tragic, either.

LEONA

(*Sharply*)

Considering your voyage the other night, I don't think we'd agree on what's funny or tragic!

JUNE

What does she mean?

LEONA

Ah, she's drunk.

JUNE

Honey—

EDDIE

I wouldn't know.

LEONA

You should. (*To* FIORIA) So should you. (*To* JUNE) So should you. You don't get it. That's 'cause I'm deep. "Just like a chasm." That's a song. Before your time. I'm before everybody's time including my own. *When does it get to be my time?*
(*She turns away. Pause.*)

EDDIE
(*Nicely*)
Come on, Leona. Don't you think you've had enough?

LEONA

No, I don't and don't be so damn patronizing! (*She puts her glass down and says very quietly:*) Mauro, go home. Cookie's gotten very unpleasant. (*Putting hors d'ouevres on a plate*) Here. Take these with you but bring back the plate.

MAURO

Thank you.
(*Goes out rear door.*)

LEONA

Can't afford to lose my buddy. Else I ain't got no buddy. Joke. Pardon. No buddy thinks any buddy's funny. Mauro would. Mauro's a prince *among thieves!*

FIORIA
(*Gets up*)
Miss Samish . . . !

EDDIE

Pay no attention.

FIORIA

No one has been a thief!

JUNE

That's a rotten crack no matter how tight you are!
(*The last three speeches are practically simultaneous.*)

LEONA

Why do you all shout at me? I didn't mean about money.

EDDIE
(*Takes* JUNE'S *hand*)

Let's go.

LEONA
(*To* JUNE)

Ask them! They know what I meant.

JUNE

Ask *them?*

. EDDIE
(*Pulls her toward house*)

Let's go!

LEONA

Yes, go! Only don't go to the movies, cookie! That's your
trouble. You go to the movies when there's a double feature
in your own backyard—

EDDIE

Can we please go?

LEONA
(*Riding right through*)

Complete with gondola—

EDDIE

That's enough!
(*Pause;* LEONA *turns away.*)

JUNE

Honey, what is she talking about?

EDDIE

Nothing! Come on!

JUNE

What does she mean?

EDDIE

Nothing. She's plastered.

LEONA
(*Holding* JUNE)
Yes, she is. I'm talking through my drinks, cookie. It doesn't mean a thing. Not a thing!

JUNE
(*Shaking her off*)
Honey, tell me that you love me. Say that you love me.
(*Goes to him.*)

EDDIE

June . . .

JUNE

Say that you love . . .
(*But she never finishes, for she begins to cry and runs past him into the house.*)

EDDIE

June, wait . . .

(*He goes in after her as:*)

LEONA

(*Calling to them*)

I made it up! I made it all up! (*But they are gone before her words are finished. In shame, she covers her face.* FIORIA *stares at her, then walks over and yanks her hands down*) I was hurt. I wanted to hurt everybody else.

FIORIA

You were hurt? By yourself! *You* threw out Di Rossi! He only wants money? You think so because you think so much of money and so little of yourself. *I* am older; *I* have half as much money; but I have twice as much men! *They* do not think of money because *I* do not think of money. And if in a few years they do, I will not throw them out. Oh, that is crude, vulgar, immoral, anh? You know why you threw out Di Rossi? Because he is not your dream of perfection. That dream, that ideal does not exist, Miss Samish. It never did, it never will! And never this way! (*Starting to clean up table*) You were hurt. *You* were— (*Slams down a plate*) You are the hostess. Clean up your own damn mess.

(*And she strides into the house.*)

LEONA

(*Rises*)

I'm sorry! (*A second, then most of the lights in the garden go out. She takes a step toward the house, holding out her arms as though to all of them*) Everybody, I'm sorry! (*Her answer is the sharp slam of the Pensione door. A pause, then she speaks quietly*) That's rude, Signora, that's very impolite . . . (*She has begun to collect the glasses, carefully pouring the remnants of martinis into one glass. Reassuring herself*) No. Everybody loves you, Leona. *Loved*. Past tense, prego. Everybody *loved* you, Leona. Grazie. Everybody—but *you*, Leona. (*She raises the now-full glass of leftover martinis but in sudden rage, hurls it against the canal wall*) Everybody! (*From the canal comes "Gondola, Gondola!" She turns to it, savagely*) Yah yah—gondola, gondola! (*Again the cry: "Gondola, Gondola!"*) I want to go home! It's wrong here, you're all wrong! And I'm right! (*Weaving in and out of the few lights*) I'm Leona Samish. I *am* attractive. I'm bright and I'm warm and I'm nice! So *want me!* Want me! . . . (*Her voice cracks on this last and she begins to cry softly*) Oh, why couldn't you love me, Renato? Why couldn't you even just *say* you loved me?

Curtain

ACT TWO

SCENE III

Morning. Although it is not very early, light only streaks the garden. The sun has not yet cleared the surrounding buildings. An occasional chime sounds, but it is quiet.

EDDIE, FIORIA *and* SIGNOR DI ROSSI *are finishing coffee and rolls.*

DI ROSSI

You think Leona is still asleep?
(FIORIA *shrugs.*)

EDDIE

June was so dead to the world, I didn't have the heart to wake her.

FIORIA
(*Acidly, to* DI ROSSI)
Americans are very considerate husbands.
(EDDIE *gets up.*)

DI ROSSI
(*Trying to lighten the atmosphere*)
Well, it is marvelous they sleep like children.

FIORIA

They are children.

EDDIE
(*Trying to be pleasant*)
We think you're children.

161

FIORIA

At least we are children with happy childhoods!

EDDIE

She's just angry this morning.

FIORIA

I am sure your wife will be singing.

EDDIE

She won't be angry.

DI ROSSI
(*Brightly*)
I myself was up very early to arrange . . .

FIORIA
(*Ignoring this, to* EDDIE)
No fight last night?

EDDIE

No fight.

FIORIA

Peccato! Tsk tsk tsk.
    (DI ROSSI, *embarrassed, gets up and starts toward the*
    house.)

FIORIA

Where are you going?

DI ROSSI

To—(*Smiles at* EDDIE)—as you would say, to wash my
hands. Scusi.
    (*Goes inside.*)

EDDIE

Look: I never lied to you. I told you I loved my wife.

FIORIA

Yes, you told me you loved . . .

EDDIE

Quit that repeating routine!

FIORIA

I should say nothing. I should be mournful in silence.

EDDIE

No . . .

FIORIA

Yes, I should. Tutto finito! There is no need to tell me. Before it even began, I knew the finishing would be quick. I accepted that. But because I accept, does not mean I like it.

EDDIE

What do you want me to do?

FIORIA

It would be terrible if I told you. (*Changing; pointing toward house*) No. I'm not going to join that chorus: Love me—want me—give me. From the day I opened this Pensione, I heard them cry, "How I give: Give love, give money, give myself" . . . "Give love, give money, give myself." These givers are takers. They only give in exchange. Only if they are insured they will get. And that is taking. Greedy children —they will end with nothing . . . And what do I end up with? Il Signor Faustino. But him I have.

EDDIE

Did I mean anything to you?

FIORIA

Now, now; you love your wife. Don't you?

EDDIE

. . . She loves me so much.

FIORIA

What a terrible thing to say! Don't be grateful for love.

EDDIE

I'm not.

FIORIA

And don't feel obligated because of it.

EDDIE

I don't.

FIORIA

Then what *do* you feel?

EDDIE

All right, both! And more. Why not? What's wrong? There isn't that much love lying around. And only her love has made us last this long. I'm going to make it work.

FIORIA

Bravo. You will be everything she wants from now on. Even pure.

EDDIE

If you really love, how can you be unfaithful? You shouldn't want anyone else. If you're married, you shouldn't have anyone else.

FIORIA

I often wonder what would have happened to Romeo and Juliet had they *not* died. (*Smiles; then:*) I am not cynical. I really agree with you. One should be faithful. I believe one cannot live without an ideal. Only . . .

EDDIE

Say it.

FIORIA

I think perhaps your way is to shut your eyes and pretend you are living the ideal.

EDDIE

What's your way?

FIORIA

To make myself see what is here and now; then to accept it, pleasant or unpleasant; and then to try to make it a little sweeter, a little closer to what I would like it to be.

EDDIE

Does that work?
(*A moment.*)

FIORIA

(*Looks at him*)
Even at this moment, I think I am happier than you. (*They smile at each other*) You smile?

EDDIE

In America, it's a sin not to smile.

FIORIA

Here, we say: you can be the greatest sinner if you have
a pure smile.

EDDIE

Mine must be angelic.

FIORIA

No: wistful—and very appealing.

EDDIE

Thank you.

FIORIA

Prego.
(JUNE *comes out of the house, very neatly dressed. She
sees them and stops short.*)

EDDIE

Good morning!

JUNE

Good morning.

EDDIE

When'd you get up?

JUNE

Not long after you left.

DI ROSSI
(*Entering behind her*)

Good morning!

JUNE

Good morning.

DI ROSSI

I trust you slept well.

JUNE

Like I was hit on the head.

EDDIE

Sit down.

JUNE

(*Ignoring him, to* DI ROSSI)
How did you make out with Mr. Papini last night?

DI ROSSI

(*Sizing up the situation*)
I told them already. We had breakfast together, the three of us.

JUNE

Well, tell me.

DI ROSSI

Everything I wanted to say to Leona, I said to Papini. He became so confused and frightened that he was finally trying to give me earrings to match the necklace!

EDDIE

I said he should have taken them.

JUNE

(*To* EDDIE, *coldly*)

Did you?

DI ROSSI

It will be much better simply to return the necklace.

FIORIA
(*To* JUNE)
Would you like your coffee, Mrs. Yaeger?

JUNE
I've had it already, thank you.

EDDIE
Why didn't you come down?

JUNE
I was busy packing.

EDDIE
Packing.

JUNE
The Contessa phoned this morning. I tried to find you . . .

EDDIE
I went for a walk. By myself. What'd she want?

JUNE
Those friends who were staying with her left for Florence so
she invited us. I didn't know where you were—

EDDIE
But you thought—

JUNE
(*After a pause. To* FIORIA)
I'm sorry not to have given you more notice.

FIORIA
That's perfectly all right.

JUNE
It'll save us a lot of money, Eddie.

EDDIE

It's done.

JUNE

She has that wonderful studio for you to work in—

EDDIE

And a houseful of idiots.

JUNE

She did say an English writer might be coming, a young English writer. But don't worry. He's never been in Venice before so while you work, I'll show him around.

EDDIE

June, don't.

JUNE

Don't what, dear?

EDDIE

Don't get even!

FIORIA

(*After a pause*)

I think she is being very wise, Eddie.

DI ROSSI

(*Gets up. To* FIORIA)

Do you think I could wash my hands again?

EDDIE

Don't be silly. Just letting off steam. (*To* JUNE) I apologize, baby.

(DI ROSSI *sits down.*)

JUNE

Honey, if it doesn't work out, we don't have to stay there. I just thought it would be better if we moved.

EDDIE

You're right.

JUNE

Poor Signor Di Rossi! I'll bet you're wondering what all this is about!

DI ROSSI

Frankly, I was thinking of my own difficulties.

EDDIE

(*Looking at the doorway*)

Well, here they come now!

(DI ROSSI *gets up. And* LEONA *enters wearing the dress we first saw her in. Now, however, it is bright and clean like the sun which is shining warmly into the garden. The city sounds are coming alive too.* LEONA *approaches the others, then turns right around and starts back, saying:*)

LEONA

No guts.

EDDIE

(*As the others laugh*)

We won't eat you.

LEONA

(*Facing them*)

I brushed my teeth four times . . . Fellas, I could kill myself or go on the wagon—which is the same thing. I'm—oh, I'm so ashamed and so sorry. Can you please forgive me?

(*There is the slightest pause, then* EDDIE *goes over to her saying:*)

EDDIE

Sure. Now that wasn't so bad, was it? Come sit down.

FIORIA
Have you had your coffee?

LEONA
No.

FIORIA
(*Bellows*)
Giovanna!

LEONA
Renato . . .

DI ROSSI
(*Smiles*)
Good morning.

LEONA
Good morning. (*To* JUNE) Cookie . . .

JUNE
Any hangover?

LEONA
(*Shaking her head*)
There's no justice in this world. I even slept like a newborn
babe.
(*A moment.*)

EDDIE
June, is there a carton or something I can pack my junk in?

JUNE
I left a box on the bed.

LEONA
You're not leaving?

EDDIE

Just moving. We're shifting over to the Contessa's.

LEONA

Oh.
(*She sits with her head down as* JUNE *follows* EDDIE *toward the house.*)

JUNE

Do you want any help?

EDDIE
(*At door*)

No, thanks.

JUNE

Honey . . . we don't have to stay there at all if you don't want.

EDDIE

We might as well take a crack at it.

JUNE

All right.

EDDIE

Don't worry, baby.
(*Goes in.*)

LEONA

I did it all with my little hatchet tongue.

JUNE

It wasn't you, or anyone else. It's, well, like I told you: if he weren't upset about his work, there wouldn't have been a thing. Not a thing. Some men turn to liquor.

LEONA

And some women do, too. (GIOVANNA *has come out with
coffee. She is sullen and silent as she turns to put down the
coffee*) Buon giorno.
(GIOVANNA *glares in answer and slides rather than
serves* LEONA's *cup to her.*)

DI ROSSI
(*As* GIOVANNA *goes*)
She is not talking at all this morning.

FIORIA

No, but she's not singing either, thank God.

LEONA

Thank me, you mean.

JUNE
(*At door*)
Well . . .

LEONA
(*Gets up, goes to her*)
June . . .

JUNE

I have to empty the medicine chest, Leona. I always save
that for the last. I'll see you. We'll both see you. Excuse me.
(*Goes into the house.*)

LEONA

I can clear a house quicker than mumps. (*Turning to*
FIORIA) I'm great for your business.

FIORIA
(Gathering the empty cups)
A Swiss couple arrives this afternoon and, tomorrow, two
Englishmen.

LEONA
Straight out: do you want me to leave?
(Sits down.)

FIORIA
Drink your coffee and stop taking so much credit. You only
made it happen one day sooner. *(Bellows)* Giovanna!
(She goes into the house.)
(Alone, both DI ROSSI *and* LEONA *are slightly uneasy. He
smiles at her, comes to table, she smiles back.)*

LEONA
Ever since I woke up, I've been wanting to see you alone.
Now I'm embarrassed.

DI ROSSI
You shouldn't be. I shouldn't be, either.

LEONA
Are you?

DI ROSSI
A little. It's going away.

LEONA
I certainly never thought I'd be having breakfast with you.
I think too much anyway. Oh, Renato, I made such a stew
over nothing.

DI ROSSI
A hundred dollars is not nothing.

LEONA

It was really the ten thousand lira for the necklace that
sent me off. Do you know how much that is? Seventeen
dollars—maybe! Seventeen dollars and I . . .

DI ROSSI

Listen. I saw the black-market man. He will exchange the
notes for you. He was so surprised, so innocent!
(*Gets up.*)

LEONA

You're not going?

DI ROSSI

Well, I must soon. Vito is not very good in the shop.

LEONA

We're so formal today.

DI ROSSI

Are we? No.

LEONA

Are you angry?

DI ROSSI

No.

LEONA

You were last night.

DI ROSSI

Not now.

LEONA

Renato, I had too much to drink

DI ROSSI

(*Smiles*)

I suspected that.

LEONA

You're really not angry?

DI ROSSI

No.

LEONA

You're something.

DI ROSSI

What?

LEONA

I don't know. Maybe I'm just self-conscious about last night.

DI ROSSI

Go swimming today.

LEONA

You sound like a doctor.

DI ROSSI

Oh, forbid!

LEONA

Well, a friend, then.

DI ROSSI

I am a *friend*.

LEONA

(*Looks at him curiously*)

You mean that.

DI ROSSI

Yes.

(*A moment. She has become very nervous.*)

LEONA

(*A pause*)

Why, Renato?

DI ROSSI
(*Moves away*)

It happens.

LEONA
(*Gets up, following him*)

Because of seventeen dollars. Because I was so stupid to let it matter, you mustn't . . .

DI ROSSI

It is not that.

LEONA

Then what?

DI ROSSI

Leona . . .

LEONA

At least, tell me!

DI ROSSI
(*Turns*)

Because I am simply too old for all this, too old and too tired and, carissima, forgive me, you are too complicated. We do not live very long but all this arguments, this explaining, this convincing, convincing, Leona, it makes life even shorter! Another man, I am used to; sometimes, no money, no place to go, even no gondola. But with you—cara Leona, with you the complication is you yourself and—it is too much!

LEONA
(*After a moment, trying to joke*)

Wore you down, eh?

DI ROSSI
(*Smiles gently*)

I am afraid so.

LEONA
(*Moves away*)
Well, I might take an ad: American lady at liberty. Has gondola. Will travel. (*Suddenly*) Please go.

DI ROSSI
(*Goes to her*)
There is another thing—

LEONA
Go please.

DI ROSSI
Unfortunately—Leona, the necklace.

LEONA
(*Turns and looks at him*)
You want it back.

DI ROSSI
It must have bad associations for you. Perhaps if we returned it—

LEONA
Thank you, no.

DI ROSSI
To keep it—

LEONA
I'll pay Papini the rest.

DI ROSSI
I could not let you.

LEONA
If it's the money you paid him, you want, I'll—

DI ROSSI
No, no!

LEONA

I want the necklace!

DI ROSSI

Leona!

LEONA

(*Almost crying*)

I've got to take *something* home from Europe!
(*Turns away.*)

DI ROSSI

And, of course, it must be a something you can touch!
That is so important! Do you know, my dear, the one time,
the only single one time when you were *not* suspicious of me?
(*Walks around to face her*) When I gave you that necklace!
When I gave you a gift, something you could touch, some-
thing that *cost!*

LEONA

(*Moving away*)

Please don't!

DI ROSSI

(*Follows her*)

Oh, yes! That was an insult, but I did not get insulted.
(*Quickly holding her*) I'm so sorry, cara, I'm sorry. I'm sorry,
forgive me. I am such a big liar. I *was* insulted then and last
night, and the anger had to get out of me. I said those words
only—oh, now, what for? What for?

LEONA

I don't blame you, cookie. I didn't mean to say cookie.
(*They smile at each other. He starts to draw away but
she holds to him.*)

DI ROSSI

I don't blame you.

LEONA

I won't be complicated, any more.

DI ROSSI

(*Gently*)

But Leona, you are. You are sure only of *things*. Of people, of living, you paint pictures in your head.

LEONA

But it's just for such a short time, Renato. Couldn't we start again? (*Goes to him*) We could pretend we just met. Come sta, Signor Di Rossi?

DI ROSSI

A little tired, Signorina.

LEONA

There's a concert in Piazza San Marco questa sera. They're playing Puccini, all Puccini. You like Puccini. Ah, please, I'm so ready now. I'm out on a limb and I'm glad to be there!

DI ROSSI

Leona . . .

LEONA

I know you. I know you're not the moon and I don't ask it any more. It's just that I have so much love in me now, I want to let it out. Let me . . .

DI ROSSI

Leona, I'm sorry. The *feeling* is gone. (*She crumples. Softly*) What can I do?

LEONA

Niente, cookie. Niente at all.

(*There is a bright cry of "Good morning, kiddos" as* MAURO *runs happily into the garden from rear door, with* FIORIA'S *platter in his hands.*)

DI ROSSI

Good morning.

(MAURO *looks at* LEONA *who is turned away from him and goes up to her.*)

MAURO

Good morning.

LEONA

Good morning.

MAURO

See? I bring plate.

LEONA

Good for you.

MAURO

But we eat food.

DI ROSSI

Take the plate inside to the Signora.

MAURO
(*To* LEONA)

Yes?

LEONA

Please.

MAURO

You be here?

LEONA

I be here.

MAURO

Okey-dokey. (*Starts to house, then turns*) Everything great, lady?

LEONA

Everything great.

MAURO

Okey-dokey.
(*Goes in.*)

DI ROSSI
(*Holding out his hand*)

Well, Leona . . .

LEONA
(*Turns to him*)

Renato—did you ever want me?

DI ROSSI

But of course!

LEONA

We're not going to see each other again, so you can say.

DI ROSSI
(*Gently*)

You would only believe me if I said I did not. But, I can tell you this: I am a man who cannot find pleasure without affection. For you I shall always have affection. (*He holds her hand in both of his a moment, then kisses it*) Adio . . .

LEONA

Good-bye?

DI ROSSI

Yes.

LEONA

Adio.

(*She watches him leave, then raises the hand he kissed to her cheek. From the house comes the voice of* GIOVANNA *singing loudly but wordlessly: "Would You Like to Take a Walk?" Suddenly,* LEONA *turns the hand over her face and cries softly.* MAURO *runs out, sees her and stops. He stands forlornly, wanting to say or do something. Finally, he comes to her and taps her politely on her arm.*)

MAURO

Upstair, a lady is crying, too.

LEONA
(*Going to her bag*)

It's Wednesday. All good Americans cry on Wednesdays. (*From the house* FIORIA *bellows: "Giovanna!" The singing stops.*)

MAURO

You wanna go see Galeria Academia?

LEONA

I don't think so.

MAURO

I very good guide for you.

LEONA

I know you are.

MAURO

Then why you no wanna see Academia?

LEONA

I'm going home, cookie.

MAURO

To America? (*She nods; she cannot talk. Sadly, after a moment:*) Okey-dokey.

> (*He looks at her, then forlornly walks toward the canal door as she gathers up her bag. Then he stops, turns and watches as she starts to the Pensione entrance. His hand reaches into his back pocket and he says:*)

Here. Parker '51.

LEONA

> (*Turning to him; smiles*)

No, thanks, Mauro.

MAURO

> (*Coming closer*)

But this no cost you nothing. Is from me! Present.

LEONA

Why?

MAURO

Ah, lady . . .

> (*Tears blur her eyes for a moment. Then she drops her bag on chair, holds out her arms. He comes to her and she hugs him close.*)

LEONA

Maybe some day, I'll just say thank you. (*Releasing him*) O.K. We go to Academia.

MAURO

Academia molta bella!

LEONA

Si. In Italy, everything molta bella!
She is trying to smile again as

The Curtain Falls